T0167914

DEAR MS EXPAT

Dear
Ms Expat

Inspiring Tales From Women Who Built New Lives In A New Land

Sushmita Mohapatra
Savitha Venugopal

Marshall Cavendish
Editions

Published by Marshall Cavendish Editions
An imprint of Marshall Cavendish International

A member of the
Times Publishing Group

Other Marshall Cavendish Offices:
Marshall Cavendish Corporation. 99 White Plains Road, Tarrytown NY 10591-9001, USA • Marshall Cavendish International (Thailand) Co Ltd. 253 Asoke, 12th Flr, Sukhumvit 21 Road, Klongtoey Nua, Wattana, Bangkok 10110, Thailand • Marshall Cavendish (Malaysia) Sdn Bhd, Times Subang, Lot 46, Subang Hi-Tech Industrial Park, Batu Tiga, 40000 Shah Alam, Selangor Darul Ehsan, Malaysia

Marshall Cavendish is a registered trademark of Times Publishing Limited

National Library Board, Singapore Cataloguing-in-Publication Data

Name(s): Mohapatra, Sushmita. | Venugopal, Savitha.
Title: Dear Ms Expat : inspiring tales from women who built new lives in a
    new land / Sushmita Mohapatra, Savitha Venugopal.
Other title(s): Inspiring tales from women who built new lives in a new land
Description: Singapore : Marshall Cavendish Editions, [2017]
Identifier(s): OCN 981258434 | ISBN 978-981-4779-00-5 (paperback)
Subject(s): LCSH: Wives--Effect of husband's employment on--Singapore--
    Anecdotes. | Resilience (Personality trait)--Anecdotes. | Creative ability--
    Anecdotes. | Aliens--Singapore--Anecdotes.
Classification: DDC 305.90691095957--dc23

Printed in Singapore by Markono Print Media Pte Ltd

To the strength that pushes prams
To the grit that wins boardroom battles
To the conviction that shatters glass ceilings
To the effort that breaks stereotypes

CONTENTS

Foreword

Too often when the words "expatriate" and "woman" are used in the same sentence, a very specific caricature is invoked. This prosaic parody shows expatriate women as primarily concerned with leisure and lunching, and completely undermines the capabilities, passions and pursuits of the majority of women living overseas. Possibly the only reason such a dated perspective still exists is that it reflects the limitations society once put upon women, rather than the limitations of the women themselves.

As someone who has lived overseas for nearly 30 years, through many iterations of my own life—including breadwinner, wife, mother, entrepreneur, author and now financial educator and mentor—one thing that never fails to impress me is the resourcefulness of women.

I have known women from all walks of life and from all corners of the earth who have created businesses and charities, and launched artistic and educational projects. These endeavours often create jobs and opportunities for other women, and greatly benefit their newly adopted home countries. And unbeknownst to most, these ventures are often started with only a handful of other passionate people and, more often than not, on shoestring budgets.

This book profiles ten expatriate women and celebrates the lives and work they have created overseas. It is also a celebration of a country like Singapore that allows these types of opportunities to flourish for its expatriate community. *Dear Ms Expat* is an important resource because it reveals the challenges and difficulties of "life on the road", and yet it also inspires us, because even under the most challenging circumstances, it shows how anyone can recreate their lives in any location. It is a welcome addition to a wide body of writing done by expatriate women, and should be used as a guiding light for new expatriates or for those who want to create more meaningful experiences overseas.

Andrea Kennedy

Founder and Educator in Chief
Wiser Wealth

Introduction

Dear Ms Expat,

Packing your life into boxes and moving to a new country is never easy. Exciting, yes. Scary, a bit. A new culture, alien languages, unfamiliar flavours and unknown roads await you. A whole new world of opportunities, apprehensions, possibilities, questions—all fused into one big adventure.

Whether you are standing hesitantly at the brink of this new chapter of your life, or you have already jumped in headlong, we welcome you to the experience. It is sure to transform you as a person. You may draw your identity from your career, from your life as a homemaker or from being a citizen of a country—regardless, everything will be viewed through new lenses.

And we suggest you get the shade just right!

What may seem overwhelming initially will finally settle down to become life's routine. Or it may not. And that is where the excitement of uncertainty lies.

In the end, it is neither as easy nor as glorified as it looks. There are chaotic days, when you question whether anything makes any sense. It could be about leaving behind that cute vintage bookcase you found in a nondescript store, or it could be a complete existential crisis.

There will be weeks of self-doubt coupled with a need to hunt for familiar things (coffee, ice cream, cookies, mum's homemade muffins). Some months will sweep past, enveloping you in a spirit of hope and promise. But through this journey, there is comfort in knowing that trying circumstances beget inspiring stories.

This book tells you the success stories of ten inspiring women who chose to aspire to great heights, challenge the norm and reinvent themselves with astounding success. Hailing from different countries, their journeys are as diverse as they are similar.

The Diversity

These women have grown up on large farms in small Australian towns, the countryside in the U.S., in the comfort of warm homes in Austria or Switzerland, or in the hilly terrains of India. They have been brought up by single mums or authoritative fathers, in large families or small. In their homes, you will hear different languages—Japanese, German, English, Bengali, Lebanese and many more. They wear their battle scars well, and of that there are many—failed marriages, life-changing illnesses, or runaway teenage years.

The Similarity

As different as their journeys may have been, what binds these women together is their resilience—along with their determination to get things done, despite present or future uncertainties. They went on to set up companies, achieve unprecedented career success or create ecosystems for other women to succeed.

Our Story and Their Stories

We set up home in Singapore a few years ago, leaving behind well-thought-out career and life decisions, close-knit families, a bunch of friends and regular coffee haunts. We went through a gamut of emotions—hope one morning, despair on another. We wanted to quickly find comfort in routine while still being exploratory in spirit. We created holiday bucket lists. (You are probably nodding your head along, because you have tread these same paths.)

While making new friends (and meeting up with long lost ones), we were introduced to women who were going through similar struggles of finding new purpose, yet there were others who seemed to have aced it right away. We were intrigued. How do you set out on your own in a place so unfamiliar? Or how do you even begin scaling the ladders of corporate success when languages and cultures keep you wondering about your next move? That was when we started documenting these stories.

The experience has been enriching. Exhilarating too! The strength, the fortitude, the refreshing acceptance of self-doubts, questions and fears. We learnt, grew and looked forward to hearing their stories.

Life is right now, right here. There is no more waiting for the perfect combination of time and opportunity. If this book gives you the motivation to explore your potential, our work here is done. If it gives you the comfort of knowing that there are ways of getting past almost any obstacle, then our work is done too.

Come, meet these wonderful women with us.

Love,
Sushmita and Savitha

Mouna Aouri Langendorf

Tunisia
Founder, Woomentum

Winning in a Man's World

Tunisia, January 2011. Violence had erupted across the country after the self-immolation of a young boy, setting in motion the Arab Spring.

In a house on a quiet hillside, a young mother cradled her three-day-old baby, keeping away from the low French windows that overlooked the streets, listening warily to gunshots outside. The neighbourhood watch had cordoned off the house to keep the family safe.

The woman, a civil engineer entrepreneur, was also worried about her clients who were working with the government on large deals—a government that was now defunct with an absconding dictator, following a rather bloody *coup d'état*.

It changed the world as we knew it and it transformed Tunisia, a picturesque African country with strong European influences. And in unfathomable ways, it changed the life of Mouna Aouri Langendorf forever. After the tumultuous events of the revolution, Mouna left her country of birth.

"We were hiding with my new born child. Some malicious groups were attacking private homes and looting shops. There were gunshots around the corner. It was a highly stressful first week for us as parents," she says. Little wonder then, that when Mouna's German husband got a job offer from Singapore, they moved countries in less than three months.

"We had to think about our baby's safety. We put everything we owned in boxes. Things we had bought to do up the nursery for our baby, our photographs, lovely gifts from our friends. Our stuff is still there. We haven't had the time to go back, sort it out or pack it well. We had to leave behind so many precious memories."

It was a heart-breaking move for Mouna, who was then heading a company with a vision of helping Tunisia grow and prosper. That continues to be a dream she carries in her heart. But in the meantime, Mouna is on a mission to help other women with Woomentum, a tech platform for women-led start-ups.

Tunisia Like It Was

Mouna grew up in a modern and liberal environment in Tunisia. A world very different from what she was confronted with years later. "It is a Muslim African country, but it was very unlike what we hear and see today. The first step taken by our previous leader Habib Bourguiba, a French-educated former lawyer, when he came into power, was to liberate women. He put a third of the country's budget into education. The best thing he could do ever, for a country like ours which was small, with only five million people."

Motivated by the socio-economic environment around her and strongly influenced by her parents, Mouna set her sights on an ambitious career. "My parents were particularly open-minded. I think my father had a huge impact on me. He ensured I had a strong belief in myself and slowed me down when I became overambitious. He shaped the way I think about life, money and values." Mouna's eyes moisten as she speaks about her dad. She lost him three years ago, and the wounds of this tragic loss are still fresh.

Her mother's influence was far subtler, but lingers on in unique ways. Her mother was one of the very few Tunisian women who made it to the most prestigious high school in the country.

Despite coming from a very modest family, Mouna's grandfather had lofty ambitions for his eldest child. "He made huge sacrifices. He was very keen that my mother head to university and become a minister." Instead, she fell in love and got married at the age of 18. Mouna was born the year after. "Later, my mother saw the impact of what she had done. She had disappointed her father and she carries with her the regret of not finishing her studies and achieving any career success. I grew up seeing my mum like that. In a way, I think I have an irrational fear of not making it in my career. I want to do everything to protect myself from the same turmoil."

Drawing from her father's fierce tenacity and her mother's fear of failure, Mouna committed herself to work towards and achieve tremendous career success. "I loved mathematics, mechanics and physics and decided to get a degree in civil engineering." She was the only girl in a class of 40 boys, but that did not unnerve her or influence any of her decisions.

"My gender was never an obstacle."

This statement hangs in the air for a bit. "It was a Muslim country, but very open-minded. I have pictures of my grandmother wearing clothes like me. My mother never covered her head. We followed our traditions and religion, but there was nothing radical. Ramadan was more about family reunions. My father did his prayers but drank whiskey with his friends too."

She explains her strong beliefs: "I grew up appreciating having a religion, but without rules that limit your possibilities, separate you from other groups or differentiate you based on gender. Religion is man-made."

Homes across Borders

With the world as her oyster and her ambitions as her wings, Mouna moved to Japan to complete her master's degree. "Most Tunisians go to Europe or Canada, but I wanted to do something different. So I chose to complete my master's in engineering in Japan, on a scholarship."

It wasn't easy for her father to see his daughter head to the other side of the world for a degree. "He was devastated, but he never discouraged me. He was keen that I get exposed to a different culture and saw this as a unique opportunity for my career development."

Away from the comforts of family and friends, Mouna started building her life in Japan. She learnt the language, set up home, started working in an engineering firm, spending over seven years in the country before she headed back to Tunisia.

"I wanted to give back to my country."

She used her understanding of Japan's culture and her fluency with the language to set up her first venture, a B2B consulting office to liaise between Japanese businesses and the Tunisian government. "They were working with the government on various engineering projects. But language was a challenge and that's where I fit in like a glove."

Mouna was part of business meetings, smoothening out deal processes and ensuring that large projects take off the ground without any communication or systemic breakdown. But the revolution cut short her ambitions here. "I remember being so apologetic about leaving my Japanese clients. The Japanese value loyalty and despite their assurances, I think as a woman, I felt quite responsible." She had spent five years building her company, but had to give it all up without a thought about what she would be doing next. For an ambitious Mouna, who had planned her career so well so far, this brought immense discomfort.

Seeking an Identity in Harsh Beginnings

Mouna's relocation to Singapore with a three-month-old baby was a move she wasn't in the least prepared for. "I had no support system and had no time to do any research on Singapore. I presumed it was going to be all okay and that finding a job was going to be easy. However, it was nothing like I imagined." Mouna quickly realised that getting a job that she liked wasn't going to be a cakewalk. "I didn't know what it meant to be unemployed, not have an income or be on a dependent visa. I could sense that the fears that my mother had about not pursuing a career had begun to gnaw at me as well."

She wasn't comfortable with the title of being just an expat mother. While she enjoyed being a mum and saw it as quite honourable, she did not seek her identity from that role. "I am Mouna and I am a mum—I wasn't comfortable with that at all. I saw my role as a mum as one that was like the other roles I played—a wife, a daughter, a sister, a friend. It couldn't encompass my whole existence."

These feelings spiralled out of control, ruining everything she held dear—her relationships, her marriage. "It wrecked my confidence. It was so crazy! One day I was running my own company and speaking four languages, and the next day I felt like I was a nobody. I didn't know how to navigate through all of this without support."

While some of it could be from the lack of friends and family she yearned for in a new place, Mouna says a lot of what she felt could be attributed to postpartum depression. "A woman is the one to be compromised when she has a child. Everything changes, her body, career, everything. But as women, we are never encouraged to talk about our feelings. And this is prevalent across cultures. I think this is wrong. It doesn't have to be that way and it will take generations for this to change. But I think the first thing to do is to find a way to talk about it."

She believes this change is the need of our times. "Our daughters don't have enough role models because we don't tell them how difficult it is. They have very little idea about the sacrifices that need to be made." She firmly believes that we owe it to the next generation to talk about postpartum depression and how lethal it can be; to say that it is time women stopped being ashamed or apologetic about hormonal changes and their impact on their lives. Forthright and refreshingly honest, her passion for this need to speak up shines through.

Working her way past the emotional challenges, Mouna started rebuilding her career. An innovative and enterprising woman, she started work on an affordable housing product, which could be built in just a week and last over 30 years. But as she readied herself for the pilot project, she realised she was pregnant again. "It was a knock-out punch! I had just completed a visit to Guangzhou and brought this project together with Cambodian micro-finance institutions. And I had to shelve everything."

But this time she was more prepared to take it on. She studied for a business degree while carrying her second child and headed out to explore opportunities soon after the little one was about six months old. "Becoming a mum humbled me and changed me forever. It was brutal and I don't think it had to be that way. For instance, becoming a father wasn't such a challenging experience for my husband. He was travelling and flourishing in his career. So, having children had essentially made him more complete. I think it completed me as well, but that came much later, when things started falling into place. Until then, it was a destabilising phase."

After her own extremely tough and emotional experience, Mouna identified the need to change the ecosystem for women leaders. And that's how Woomentum was born.

Mouna's Woomentum offers networking and fundraising opportunities for women entrepreneurs.

Creating a New World for Women Entrepreneurs

While there were networking meetings, coffee catch-ups, panel discussions, events and summits (and more strength to them!), she believed that an online forum was still missing. "With women juggling so many things, I think it is tough to always meet in person. So, I wanted to create a safe place online where they could go."

Woomentum was created to provide a platform for women to browse through and learn about building a business, find advice from mentors, get coaching, or raise funds. It is an avenue for successful women entrepreneurs to provide advice to other professionals and develop mentor-mentee relationships. "Research shows that women do invest in women-led ventures. It doesn't mean they are sexist, they would invest in other ventures led by men as well. But affluent women are looking for avenues to do some angel investing to help other women."

The focus of the organisation is two-pronged. One is an expert marketplace, where a woman founder can book a slot with an expert for advice. The second one is crowdfunding. Woomentum's flagship event, CrowdFundHer Live™, helps raise money and hours for women-run businesses. The most recent one was hosted by Bloomberg and the start-ups pitched to an audience of over 200 people, which included experts from companies like KPMG and Google.

"Women don't pitch enough and that is a big problem. At accelerators and incubators, one mostly sees men. Women feel shy or out of place. It is shocking that only 4 percent of venture capitalists' money goes to women-led start-ups!"

Mouna is doing all she can to change it, drawing from her experiences of often being the only woman civil engineer in a room full of boys and men. "I want to build a digital community for women. Women don't network over Friday beers. They have different needs and ways of seeking help and funds. I want to make it easier for women to innovate."

Mouna's energy reflects in the success of the events she organises.

Dear Ms Expat,

I think there are different types of expats. There are some who want to build their careers and continue working and there are some who enjoy being at home. I have complete respect for all of them and their choices.

There are groups where women who build their homes and families can reach out to each other for advice. For women who are seeking to build their careers, I would say they need to ask for help. We women sometimes take too long to ask for assistance. Get out as fast as possible and plug into the communities of like-minded women. If you interact with the wrong people, you are subjected to judgements and unnecessary clashes.

Also, you need to be confident about who you are and be curious about what's out there. Know your skills and talk to people. I went to a co-working space for about $350 a month. For about six months I didn't have a clear mission, but I was paying that money; it was an investment I had to put in to get myself out there and grow my network. Gaining access to an entrepreneurial community can also help you find a job. You might be able to volunteer, learn new skills and perhaps set up your own business by knowing more.

It also makes you a more confident person. If you feel you want to leave the kids to the helper, so be it. Don't look at the neighbour who doesn't. Because if you start comparing, you will make the choice to sit at home, that's a no-brainer. I started pre-school for my kids early to give me flexibility and my kids are lovely and very balanced. They have never let me down.

Best wishes,
Mouna

Carolyn Soemarjono

Australia
Boudoir Photographer

Life across High Mountains and Messy Valleys

Carolyn Soemarjono buzzes around her bright and airy studio, ensuring the air conditioning is just right, the scented candles are lit, the fluttering white curtains are drawn to let in natural light and the sets are ready for the next client. As Singapore's first exclusive boudoir phorographer, Carolyn specialises in taking intimate portraits of women.

Sitting amidst stunning pictures, Carolyn knows just how far she has come from her first job in a small town in Australia. Her journey so far has been studded with adventures—the ones she went after, like traveling and hunting for new avenues; and the ones she did not see coming, like cancer. After over 20 years in corporate jobs, it was cancer that became the trigger for Carolyn to turn her passion into a career and go from being a human resources manager to a photographer.

The Turbulent Teens

Carolyn grew up on a large farm in Dubbo, Australia; a happy childhood spent amongst cattle, horses, cats and dogs. But that changed as she grew up. "As a teenager, I had a lot of issues and I fell into some bad company. I hated school and wasn't getting along very well with my parents at that time." At the earliest opportunity of leaving school with a certificate, she did, foregoing two remaining levels of high school. At 16, Carolyn had found a job and moved into an apartment all by herself. "That was a pretty rough start to my adult life."

She started work at a clothing store, which used to be her part-time gig while she was still in school. The shop gave her a full-time role and a crucial epiphany. "I had no real qualifications or training. I looked around at all the people who had been there for a decade or more and I thought to myself, I am not doing this for the next 10 years. Having that sort of attitude eventually helped me move on to learning some new skills and going to school at night."

By the time she was 18—an age at which your average teenager is thinking of high school farewell parties, college applications and summer jobs—Carolyn had worked at a few more small businesses, completed a course in accounting and moved to Sydney. It was here that she had her first exposure to a big company, as an accounting clerk with Unilever. "It was a very basic role. I kept wanting to learn and explore more."

By then, Carolyn had also reconciled with her parents. "Between 16 and 18, it was kind of rough. There were times when I barely had enough money to buy food. And funnily enough, when I was 19, I went the other way and became more responsible, more serious and quite settled," she says.

When in Doubt, Choose Hard Work

In Carolyn's studio, amongst the photography equipment and displays, there is a little poster that sums up quite well what life has been like for her: "She believed she could, so she did."

But she is quick to point out that she was just as filled with doubt as anyone else. "At Unilever, I knew that I could do the work that all these wonderful university graduates were doing. But at the same time, I also felt that since I didn't go to university, maybe I couldn't. It was the same with photography when I first thought about it. My first reaction was, oh no, I couldn't do it, you have to be an expert to be able to do all that."

The doubts did not stop her, though. Instead, she worked to move past them. And an integral part of that process was her constant lookout for new experiences. This is what took her to London at the age of 20 for a period of two years, with her boyfriend, whom she later married. During this time, she travelled through Europe and took up work on short contracts—a stint that she looks back on as an experience she cherished.

Once back in Sydney, she joined Procter & Gamble, which turned out to be a relationship that lasted 20 years. Never letting her lack of a university degree hold her back, Carolyn broke barriers and moved up the ranks, from administration to senior management. "I believe what motivates me is the desire to learn and push past the fear that usually holds us back. I still have that fear, but it is about going beyond it." This is also when she made a switch from an accounting role to human resources.

In the meantime, Carolyn had become a mother to a baby girl. But divorce followed soon after and she began a new chapter in life as a single parent.

As work picked up, so did her personal life and she started dating a colleague. However, some time soon after, he was transferred to Singapore. Much back-and-forth and complications later, Carolyn joined him with a transfer within Procter & Gamble to its new regional headquarters in the country.

"It wasn't an easy move. I had to go through counselling. I felt like the worst mother in the world, moving my daughter from her father to another country when she was only seven. With the help of a counsellor, we worked out that it was one of those things that I just had to try. What if something good happens? If you don't try, you will never know. I am so glad I took that big leap."

Her move was supposed to be a trial run for a year. "I loved living here, I loved the lifestyle and I was so happy in our relationship. That one year has now become 13!" If there was one person who took to Singapore better than Carolyn herself, it was her daughter. Carolyn remembers how well the little one thrived with the independence she had and the new life she found here.

Life settled into a great rhythm. At work, Carolyn tackled several different assignments and continued her journey up the ladder. "Often I had to fake it until I made it. Several times on assignments, you simply have to figure your way through. You ask for help and you learn as you go. And I learnt so much in that company, starting as an accounts clerk doing invoicing and such, to being a global HR leader for the skincare brand SK-II," she says.

For Carolyn, the Singapore lifestyle came with an emphasis on fitness and health. Inspired by the jogging tracks and their accessibility, she and her husband took up running, an activity that not only kept them fit but also strengthened their bond with each other.

She brought this passion to work as well, as she was managing the health and well-being programme for over 2,000 employees. "I was living and breathing healthy stuff—eating salads for lunch and running marathons. Everyone saw me as the leader of everything the company was doing to promote the health and well-being of employees.

The Game Changer

Carolyn was 42 and ran the Tokyo Marathon that year. About two months after the marathon, she could barely run 10K. Things got worse and there were days when she didn't even have the energy to go to work. "Normally, I could run 10K before going to work in the morning. And now I could barely get out of bed."

Doctors ran tests, but could find nothing wrong. It could be stress, they suggested. But Carolyn could not leave it at that. She had a nagging feeling that something was seriously wrong. One night, after a bout of nausea, Carolyn sleeplessly started searching online and came upon blogs that suggested that these could be symptoms of ovarian cancer. "This was at 2 a.m. and I thought to myself, that's what it is, I've got ovarian cancer. Next day, I went straight to the doctors. I said, you are going to think I am a hypochondriac, but I think I've got ovarian cancer."

Very soon, they found the cancer. Carolyn was in surgery and was then put through a rigorous treatment that required her to go through chemotherapy once a week for 18 weeks. "They said, we are going to take out your ovaries and uterus; you are going to go straight into menopause. I had a meltdown! My husband and I wanted to have children together. That was really tough. That's when we got the cats. That helped," she says with a laugh.

Life during chemotherapy was a blur. She spent her days on the sofa watching television series. She barely went out. She took it as her job to go through treatment and just get better. Through the months of treatment, Carolyn says she could barely string a sentence together. "I was really a little bit out of it all. It was like being drunk all the time, but not in a good way."

Her family formed her support system, with her husband being the doting caretaker, working from home and taking her to the chemotherapy sessions, and her 17-year-old daughter taking it all in her stride and being strong for her mother. She found that if you had the money for it, or an insurance policy that covers it, you could get truly world-class medical care in Singapore, with a team of doctors who have trained at reputed universities across the world.

Carolyn also found help at the Expat Cancer Support Group, a group in which she is an active member, even now. Started by two oncology nurses, who have since moved back, it works as a resource for people, to share their stories and seek help.

It took Carolyn a good two years to feel normal again after the chemical onslaught from the cancer treatment.

"I didn't feel sick during those two years, but I was so tired that every day I had to lie down in the middle of the day. I had no hair, no eyebrows, no eyelashes. I had lost all sense of balance. But sometime in those two years, I started running again," she says.

"Essentially, I self-diagnosed and saved my life. A lot of women die from this cancer. If I hadn't kept searching online and asking the questions, it might have been a different story. I knew that something was wrong with my body. I often tell people that if you feel something is wrong, don't just take the doctor's word for it. The doctor doesn't know you like you know you. Keep pushing till you get the answer. For me, that turned out to be the best thing I ever did."

Turning Cancer into a Catalyst

The recuperation period had also been a time of introspection. Once she was out of the grip of the disease, Carolyn wanted to turn her life around. She saw it as a chance to make sure that cancer became the best thing to have happened to her, to make it the catalyst for a better life.

The first step towards it was to cut stress out of her life. Convinced that that was what caused her cancer in the

Carolyn makes it a point that both she and her client enjoys the shoot.

first place, she did not want to go back to a stressful job. Also, by then she was not a good fit for the company, given how they wanted her back on full-time employment while she wasn't yet ready for that. It was time for yet another difficult decision for Carolyn—to quit a job she had had for about two decades.

During her recovery, she had been dabbling more and more in photography. It was a colleague who planted the idea that she could take it up as a profession. "One of my friends wanted a family portrait taken, and I went and did it for her. I was telling her how I wasn't sure about going back to the corporate life, about doing something different. And she said, why don't you become a photographer? My first reaction was that I am not a photographer, I am an HR manager!"

But having quit her HR job, she soon started doing more photography and was surprised that people were actually paying her to do something she loved. Carolyn was soon becoming quite successful in family photography with a speciality in portraits, but she realised that her passion lay in photographing women.

"I used to have a lot of people come to my home for headshots for social media, mostly women. I would spend two hours with them just to get one good photo because that's often how long it took to get them relaxed and natural. I always loved portraits but I hadn't realised that I particularly loved women's portraits. That is when I started thinking about boudoir photography."

She also recalled her 40th birthday, when she wanted to do a boudoir photo shoot for herself but couldn't find a photographer in Singapore who would do it the way she wanted. She ended up doing her photo shoot back in Australia. She knew there was a nascent demand here. Having found her niche and seen the opportunity for it in Singapore, Carolyn decided that was what she would do.

Becoming a Boudoir Photographer

But it remained an idea for a long time until one day her friend, having decided to nudge Carolyn into acting on it, landed up with her lingerie collection ready to do a photo shoot. "During the photo shoot, I found it the most fantastic thing ever; I loved it. From that moment on, I have focused on doing boudoir photography alone. I love the whole process," Carolyn says, the joy of it evident in her voice.

Carolyn with her daughter Leah and mother Patricia.

Given how much time she puts into each client, she takes on only four a month. "I take a very limited number because I like to give a lot of personal attention. I like to meet the client first and then when she comes back for the shoot, I spend most of the day with her. I put out champagne and some snacks, carefully go through the outfits, make her feel comfortable because if they are comfortable, it shows. After the photo shoot, I review the images, picking out the ones I think are the best," explains Carolyn.

A Mother Again

Carolyn's life is now busy with the newest little joys in her life—two babies that Carolyn and her husband have adopted. She has become a grandmother as well! Her eldest daughter, who returned to Australia a few years ago to attend university, is now married and has a little baby of her own.

"I think Singapore has made a most amazing impact on my life," Carolyn says. She counts off on her finger how it facilitated her relationship and helped it grow, brought on a wonderful lifestyle change and enabled her to build her business. Looking back at what her journey has been, Carolyn comments, "It is not as though I just go with whatever comes my way. These decisions and events do affect me. For a lot of people—including my husband—life is like a straight line. There are not too many big highs or lows. But mine has been full of mountains and messy valleys!"

Dear Ms Expat,

There are a lot of opportunities out there; but you've got to go and find them yourself. I do think that no matter where you are coming from, whether you are working or not working, no one is just going to bring things to you. You have to get out there, meet people, join clubs, find sporting groups—just do things, anything really—these can lead to so many social or work opportunities, some of which you may never have previously thought of.

If you are looking for work, do get involved in associations in the community. It will not only be an opportunity to attend sessions and network, but also to provide talks on topics that you have expertise in. You never know how the people you meet along the way could help you in the future.

I've certainly spent the best years of my life in Singapore and have a lot to be grateful for. I'm sure you could also benefit from the chance to form new friendships, the opportunities to learn new sports and skills, and the safety and security for your family that few countries can match.

Best wishes,
Carolyn

Danielle Warner

United States of America
CEO & Founder, Expat Insurance

The Unexpected Entrepreneur

Taking in the iconic skyline of Manhattan from a corner office, she smoothed out the folds in her crisp Chanel suit. On the desk lay her custom-made handbag and copies of the latest *Insurance Journal*. She would browse through one of them, reminiscing about the time when she was a newbie in this field. The climb up the corporate ladder had been swift and steady.

This is how Danielle Warner had imagined her life in her 30s would be. Never had she thought that she would achieve so much more. Sure, the view from her window is different, but no less spectacular.

Danielle is the CEO and Founder of Expat Insurance, a company that services 25,000 private clients and about 12,000 members of corporate clients on a global scale.

Her office overlooks Clarke Quay, the historic riverside quay named after Singapore's second governor Andrew Clarke. She has traded her Chanel suit for a formal summer dress. Insurance magazines stack up at the reception of her own office, sharing space with lifestyle magazines that have Danielle on the cover, and her own book, *Bulletproof.*

"I never thought I was going to be an entrepreneur. But somewhere quite early on, I got really connected with what I do. I go back to the 'why are you doing it' question very often. And the cause is important. I have expertise in the insurance sector and I wanted to build something for the expatriate community," says Danielle. Her smile is wide, confident and reassuring, and her enthusiasm for her business, almost child-like and infectious.

Sure about Insurance

Danielle grew up in the Pocono mountains of Pennsylvania, in a small town called Dingmans Ferry. "When I tell someone that I grew up in the mountains, no one is ever able to comprehend how mountainous the region is. My mother still lives there, off a dirt road, which is quite unlike the U.S."

Brought up in a single-parent household, Danielle imbibed two things very early in her life: a love for travel and the art of enjoying work—both from her Hungarian Catholic mother. "My mother always had a keen focus on travelling. It was nowhere exotic, because there were financial constraints. But we travelled quite a bit within the U.S., or went on a cruise, wherever we could go, and took holidays that gave her some downtime as well."

Danielle's mother worked as part of the senior leadership in AIG and it was this world of insurance that Danielle had great familiarity with, from her childhood. "My whole family works in insurance, my mum, my aunt, my cousins, everyone. I have known about the sector since very early days." And while others may perceive it as being drab or boring, Danielle thought otherwise. "My mum loved her work, from the moment she woke up to when she went to sleep. And I do too."

It was little surprise then that AIG is where she headed for her summer job. "I enrolled in the Pennsylvania State University, but felt like just a number in the mammoth campus of 80,000 students. I moved to a smaller 1,200-strong liberal arts college in Florida. I used to fly back every summer from there, to make the two-hour commute to New Jersey with my mother and work as an intern at AIG."

She started out in the file room, moving up to work as an assistant underwriter with some relationship building responsibilities. With so many summers of experience under her belt, after college, she joined the leading insurance player in the marketing and communications department.

It was the small-town girl's big dream come true—landing her first job in Manhattan.

Destiny Changes the Course of Dreams

All of 21 when she graduated from college, Danielle met her future husband, a British colleague in the company's international division, just a year later. It was a whirlwind romance of three months, after which he moved to Singapore. "I decided not to follow him because I was doing my dream job! I had just got promoted, my mum was proud of me and I was following the family line," says Danielle, sounding very much like the young adult she was.

She may not have followed him across the world, but that didn't mar their relationship. "He continued to court me, flew me to Asia and took me for a holiday to Bali, giving me a glimpse of what life as an expat would be like."

The expat lifestyle in Singapore a decade back was very different from what it is now. "It was all very enticing for the 23-year-old me. You never saw a bill in your life and the company took care of everything."

Danielle decided to stay, a decision that wasn't easy to make. "All I could think of was, 'How will I convince mum? It is not going to be okay.'"

She took to heart the advice given by her girlfriend, who said, "You must see it as an adventure at 23. If you don't do it now, you will regret it. You are at a stage in your life where if it goes all wrong, you can come back and your career won't be destroyed." And surprisingly, Danielle's mother supported her move too. It's an adventure that played out rather well.

A Turbulent Start

"I felt that Singapore showed me who I really am as a woman. I had to create an identity because what do you really know at 23? Whatever you do know, you need to re-learn anyway. I have had an interesting experience, because I had to build something for myself here."

It wasn't a journey without its challenges, of course. "I didn't come in with a job. Unfortunately, AIG didn't have a marketing and communications role in Singapore at that point. It was in Hong Kong. So there I was—with just a tourist visa and no job."

After a hectic year of travelling and networking, Danielle picked up her first job. She joined the Swiss Education Group that owned hospitality universities in Switzerland. Singapore was on the cusp of a huge hospitality boom as the country's iconic Marina Bay Sands had been commissioned, but not built yet. "Singapore was heavily investing to bring up a talent pool that could sustain this industry and the company was looking at recruiting Asian students for these hospitality courses." Danielle took on multiple roles at this organisation for about a year.

"And then I got bored." She hit a tough emotional patch after being in the country for two years. "I wanted to rebuild my career that had started so well in New York. I wasn't feeling very fulfilled here and really struggled as a woman who was in Singapore without being married."

Danielle voices the challenges that many an expat partner faces when she lands in Singapore. She says that there is an expectation that here you will be able to recreate what or where you came from. "Everyone expects it. But that never happens." Danielle's voice softens. She had seen this emotional upheaval in so many lives.

Soon after though, things started looking up. On a visit to an art gallery to pick up a couple of pieces, Danielle met the owner, British entrepreneur Chris Churcher. A former investment banker, Chris had joined his wife in following their passion for art. Danielle started working at Red Sea Gallery, managing the gallery and working on a rebranding exercise. "It was back to my marketing days and I was excited to do it for a cool brand." Unfortunately, the tenure was cut short by the global financial crisis that impacted the business.

Turning Entrepreneur

Almost on cue, the sun blazes through the clouds after a sudden afternoon shower. Danielle's eyes light up as she tells us about her first baby.

"It was my boyfriend who came up with the idea. When we were travelling as an unmarried couple, we could never buy an insurance policy together. There wasn't a convenient way to buy it either. I remember once we ended up on an AIG Canada webpage!" Danielle realised rather quickly that finding policies was tough, even for someone who knew this inside and out.

"We were both in insurance, had worked with AIG, one of the biggest players in the sector and we couldn't find our own insurance! What are the chances that other expats could do this?" And that germinated the idea of Expat Insurance. "Let us be the people who can provide this advice!"

It didn't quite turn out like that. Her boyfriend chose to stay on at his corporate job and Danielle took on the mantle of setting up the company. She worked through visa issues and requisite professional qualifications needed to offer insurance advice. From there on, it was all about learning new skills along the way.

"First off, I had to go out and pitch to three big insurance companies to become their agent. I was just a girl with an idea—no portfolio and I had never sold insurance before! I had never sold anything before actually," she guffaws. "Apart from perhaps, my relocation to my mother."

"I Don't Believe in Balance"

Expat Insurance was officially launched on January 1, 2010. But Danielle had already tested the waters through her network built over three years. Galleries, associations, professional networks—she had covered them all and the feedback had been overwhelming.

"We started when the financial crisis was at its worst, and looking back I can't think of a better time to have set it up. Our business could adapt to the client base. Expat packages were shrinking. We could tell the big insurers that the products had to change because our client demands were evolving," she says.

As the business grew from strength to strength, so did Danielle's family. She got married in 2011 at Raffles Hotel with just 12 people on the guest list, as her business commitments didn't leave her with much time to plan a wedding.

In the next three years, Danielle had two babies, less than two years apart. Starting a family was a decision that had left her rather perplexed. She followed the advice her godmother gave her: "Stop trying to fit it in. Just let it happen! Get it done and move on. No matter where you are or what you are doing. It doesn't matter whether you've just got a promotion and you are scared about where you are going to be if you have children. You will figure it out as you go along."

And she has figured it out all right.

"I don't believe in balance. Life is all about decisions and compromises," she says with conviction. It may be a non-conformist view, but for a woman who turned into an entrepreneur when she was 25-years-old, it is a view that works for her and helps her succeed. "When I am with my babies, I am not with my business. And that is my baby too! I think deciding priorities is important. If things are not going well at work, and your children are not well, where do you want to be?"

Danielle also stays away from playing into the mothers' guilt syndrome. She accepts that it crept in after she stopped breast-feeding her first child. "But I realised soon enough that women will always have a sense of guilt that follows them. And I decided that if I had to be guilty about something, then I would let it be about something big. There really isn't a point being guilty about all the little things. If you are not going to be with your kids, let it be for doing something that you also really want to be doing."

The Changing Face of Business

Danielle had started the business selling only products from three companies. But along the way, to provide unbiased advice, Expat Insurance procured more licenses and turned into an independent brokerage. This was core to what Danielle and her husband had set out to do.

As the business landscape evolved, it became even more crucial. "The demand has changed entirely in the 12 years I have been here. Earlier it was about insuring jewellery, because that was the only thing that the employer didn't cover. But now expats know that the employer doesn't typically cover comprehensive healthcare, and even if they do, it is not likely to be enough."

As the expat needs changed, so did the face of Expat Insurance. Danielle's husband quit his corporate job in 2015. He helped steer the business towards a significant change in course. Expat Insurance had begun acquisition talks with the fourth largest insurance player in France and he was leading the due diligence and legal processes for the deal. "This perhaps then is a story, where you come in as the trailing partner, but then set up a company and a source of income that sustains the family. It has been quite a journey."

In April 2016, the acquisition process was complete and Expat Insurance was acquired by MSH International. "We had been getting offers frequently, because the business was doing so well and it was so niche. I thought they would be the best partners. We were not being forced into rebranding. Our brand stays. I maintain unlimited tenure as CEO and have complete management control. And the terms are very, very good as we continue to remain shareholders. I also like their hands-off approach and entrepreneurial spirit. I didn't sell out; I am not done yet."

"I wanted to build something for the expatriate community."

Dear Ms Expat,

Think of yourself first and be a little selfish. It may sound controversial, but I have seen so many women head down the dark path in their expat lives. That is because they do not share their emotional state with their husbands, for fear of adding more stress to their plate. Their focus is to be there for the kids.

If you are not fulfilled and happy yourself, how can you be the best support that you can be for your marriage, family, friends or people back home? Be a little selfish, to ably support your children. It is okay to think about yourself as a priority and seek happiness and fulfilment.

I also love this advice that I received when I came in here: stay humble and be true to yourself. We are living in the echelons of wealth that most of us have never experienced in our childhood. It is so easy to get lost here, between champagne brunches, Orchard shopping and fancy rooftop bars. We get so caught up in this life because you don't meet people who you know from way back and who can keep you grounded. Staying true to yourself is important for the children.

Best wishes,
Danielle

Angelina Grass-Oguma

Austria

Partner, Oliver Wyman

Scripting Success on Her Own Terms

They set out on long Sunday drives. Picnic baskets, stories and her favourite people. These journeys were special. They came with anecdotes of lands far and wide; of a life lived miles away from Austria. Fairy tales come in different shapes and forms and for this little girl, they were the tales her father told of his life of adventure as a young immigrant in Canada. Seeds of future dreams were sown on those weekend excursions. Not just of trying out new things, but much more.

For Angelina Grass-Oguma, a senior partner at Oliver Wyman, her sheltered upbringing with a spiritual mother, an ambitious businessman father and a sibling shaped how she paved her journey into the big, bad world.

"Growing up with these stories about my father's life as

an expat opened me up to the idea of going abroad," she reminisces. Angelina was all of 13 when he took her on one of his business trips, showed her around the places he lived and got her to meet his friends. And there it was, the excitement he experienced in real life. "I got a glimpse of his lifestyle there." She was hooked.

An Early Start

Angelina brings to the conference room a quiet confidence and visible warmth. She is prepared with a set of notes, a wristwatch to track time and the openness to talk about her life experiences. A life where her journey across the seas began early.

A grade A student, she is unabashedly proud of her ambition and will to succeed. "I was always trying to reach for the top," she recalls. A lot of this, she believes, is drawn from her experience as a toddler, trying to get attention from her father. "For me to be smarter than my brother, who is older by a year, was tough. I was constantly trying to outdo him. Do math faster or write better. I had to be better and I had to shine!"

This dogged determination has taken her places. At high school in Austria, she did five grades in four years and then she was off to Oxford where she studied Philosophy, Politics and Economics for three years. At just 22, she joined her first (and current) employer Oliver Wyman, right out of campus.

And now, she is one of the most successful partners in the international consulting firm. "I am a mother of two, I work part-time and I am among the highest-paid partners at Oliver Wyman," she says matter-of-factly. If you've wondered what success on your own terms looks like, Angelina wrote that script.

Building a Home in Asia

As a consultant, Angelina worked with clients across regions. While she had been recruited for the Frankfurt office, she was soon in Australia working for a project. From there she moved to Bangkok. A transfer to Asia seemed like an obvious choice. "My father wasn't too keen about my move, despite his own experience as an expat when he was young. He was most worried about me marrying an Asian." A premonition that came true, soon after.

Angelina's Asian journey began with a lot of travel to explore the region, for work and leisure. However, she was still struggling to make friends here.

"Although my head office was in Singapore, I spent most of my week in Bangkok. That made making friends quite tough." She used some of the free time on her hands to start learning Japanese. And that played a part in her choosing someone to share her flat with, when she finally set up home in the island country. "I can get some help with my Japanese!" she thought, when selecting a Japanese young man to look for shared accommodation together. They met in 2006, soon became a couple, and had an "ultra-minimalistic" wedding in 2009.

"We didn't want to get married at all! But in Japan, for children to get rights, you need to be registered as a married couple. My in-laws helped to get the paperwork done there and one morning at work, we got an email from my father-in-law saying 'Congratulations! You are married now. Have a happy life together!'" A tinge of amusement lingers in her smile as she talks about her wedding. They did take the afternoon off to celebrate and have some pictures taken. "I am happy we did that."

With her father's nightmares about her marrying an Asian coming true, gaining acceptance in her family wasn't easy. There were skipped Christmas celebrations

Angelina with her husband Tetsuya.

—and even a walkout at her brother's wedding after an argument—before her father accepted her choice. But Angelina seems rather unfazed about what she had to face and is happy to accept that she had to turn around a fairly "racist" father.

The Balancing Act

Love, relationships, careers, homes—everything had played out to script. But the decision to become a mother had her stumped.

"We wanted to have kids." But with Singapore being a regional hub and travel being so core to her job role, decisions like these came with tears and major negotiations at the workplace. "Despite my boyfriend (now husband) knowing I was supposed to travel, there was a time when he said that either I travel less, or we break up. I loved my work and I loved him. I was torn."

She went back and spoke to her seniors. They agreed to allow her to travel less, bringing it down to three days and two nights a week. "I was in tears when I explained my situation."

You win some, you lose some. While flexibility came in, the much-coveted partnership promotion did not. "The plan was to make partner and then have kids." However, the first year she was put up for partnership in the firm, she did not make it. "I remember calling my husband, very upset about this. And instead of consoling me, he was curious about the impact it would have on our plans to start a family. 'But what about the baby?!' were his exact words." Angelina smiles.

She was hugely disappointed with the turn of events, but Angelina didn't wait for her professional dream to take shape. She moved ahead and decided to start a family. And sure enough, partnership followed the year after.

Starting a Family

Not one to be cowed down by changing trends, Angelina believes in natural birth and had her two kids in the most non-intrusive way possible, at home. "I hear that this is quite rare in Singapore. But I was convinced that if I was left to do it, then I could, because my body was made for this. If no one bothered me, I was going to do it." And she did. While for her first child she had a gynaecologist at home, for her second baby, it was just her husband who helped her deliver.

Having children didn't stymie her travel or career progression. When she went back to work, she travelled every week with her first child and nanny. "I resumed work soon after giving birth and received permission to travel with my nanny and baby. Till my daughter was 14 months old, she was with me every single night of her life," she says.

Angelina's two kids are now six and four years old. She strives with her husband to bring them up with understanding and awareness of both their cultures. They are trilingual and know Japanese, English and German languages. "An immense amount of hard work has gone in to ensure that it is kept that way. Japanese kindergartens, German nannies and schools—many experts have been roped in to make it happen."

A lot of this balancing act has been possible because of her husband's support. He stays home with the kids and allows her the flexibility to change plans on short notice. "He manages it all and I am very reliant on my husband. Other women who do not have a stay-at-home husband or have husbands with demanding jobs may find it quite difficult to build a support system. We also have a housekeeper and that has been quite helpful. But being away from grandparents and away from siblings, I have been lucky to have my husband at home. And having family support was important for us," she says.

A fast talker, Angelina's convictions and beliefs come through easily. And her words keep pace with her thoughts, without a hem and a haw.

Being in a multicultural hub like Singapore also helps to ensure that the kids assimilate easily. "My father keeps saying that international marriages are not a great idea because the children will not have an identity. But I don't agree with that. The Singapore expat community has an international mindset, more religious and racial tolerance and very interesting conversations," she says.

"We were on a bus recently and the kids were asked where they were from. They said Singapore. Then they were asked where mummy is from or where papa is from? They were confused about me. Maybe Germany, they thought! And they didn't know the answer for where papa is from too. Clearly, they identify themselves as Singaporean kids." The expat community is, however, very transient; one needs to be more open to make friends.

Being a Woman and a Leader

It hasn't been easy, but Angelina has managed to achieve the enviable balance between her work and family. "I only work four days a week and don't work on weekends. I take my kids to bed and have dinner with them most days. And I am very successful at work."

She sees her success as a leader to have very little to do with her gender. "I take my gender as an advantage. I have never seen a situation where I think someone is judging me. I always had a figure-it-out or I-will-make-it-work attitude." And it sure has helped.

"A lot of women in their 20s or early 30s have questions

around how it is all going to play out. Especially since they may not have a woman they can look up to or a lifestyle they can emulate, within their organisations." Angelina faced the challenge as well, but decided to confront it head-on, asking for things that will help her work better. And she believes that is the best approach for women in similar situations. Of course, it helped that Oliver Wyman supported her along the way.

Going ahead, Angelina hopes to contribute significantly to the non-profit sector. "I have always wanted to work in the areas of poverty elimination." She is a board member in a non-profit organisation in Myanmar, but is looking for a larger role—one that hasn't come by yet. "I have not been able to take on a role in the sector, despite my passion here."

The ambitious little girl who competed with her brother for attention has now mellowed down. Achieving career success of making partner before 30 years of age gave her the emotional high of success and freed her up from the baggage of constantly striving.

Today, she is happy in her space and time. Gathering her thoughts with her eyes closed, she says, "My ambitious streak has softened over these years. I have calmed down."

Dear Ms Expat,

The expat community is very welcoming and open-minded. So, it is easy to get along and make friends. My word of advice here will be to get engaged with something very quickly. Join a cooking start-up or start volunteering at your children's schools. It is important to be challenged mentally and start feeling like Singapore is home.

There is immense ease of life in Singapore. The government has made it a point to keep it quite easy—the traffic, taxes, everything. Enjoy that!

Best wishes,
Angelina

Andrea McKenna

United States of America
Writer and Yoga Instructor

Rising from the Ashes

There are good days and bad. On the good days, she is productive, calm and happy. She works on her book, blogs and writes for the magazine where she is a regular contributor. A seasoned yoga practitioner, she also heads to the yoga studio to teach.

On bad days, things slow down and she tries to help herself with sound healing, essential oils and rest. Sometimes nothing moves; she stays in bed allowing the medication to take over and act. She may even head out to meet her therapist.

On an exceptionally bad day several years ago, she attempted to kill herself with all the medication she had at hand.

For Andrea McKenna, this is what living with bipolar disorder has been like. Having survived her worst years with the illness, she is now a voice that strives to reach as many people as possible in the hope that mental health issues will get their due and those who suffer from them get the treatment they need.

Andrea uses her passion for writing and yoga to reach out to people who may need help. As a writer, she attempts to make herself heard over the deafening silence that often surrounds mental health issues. Yoga, which she has been teaching for 17 years now, is both the ticket to her own wellness and serves as a helping hand to those going through troubled times.

She calls herself the bipolar phoenix and she couldn't have chosen a better expression to indicate how she has built her life back up.

Life as a Young Journalist

Andrea spent her childhood in the small tourist town of Mystic, Connecticut. From a fairly young age, she knew she wanted to be a writer. So when the time came, she pursued journalism at Boston University, specialising in broadcast media. She started her career quite young

Andrea during her first few months in Singapore.

too, as a radio reporter in college. Great experience and exposure came her way when she went to England for the last semester to work for a BBC contracted company.

Out of college, she landed her first job in New York on Wall Street, at a financial magazine. "It was a dream for me. I worked Monday to Friday. Thursday nights we stayed late. I would take a taxi home and while crossing the Brooklyn Bridge, I would turn around and look at the Manhattan skyline and think, yes, I have made it! I was 22 years old, I was thrilled and didn't care that I only made US$300 a week because it was New York. There was no fear, I got everything done with no one to help me. I was proud of that independence, especially coming from a small town."

But love for New York paled in comparison to the lifelong romance she began with Chicago a few years later. Andrea moved to the Windy City with a new job (again in financial media) and has since called it home. "I felt that it was the most amazing city I had ever been in my life. They have a real focus on the quality of life whereas everywhere else I had been was all about work. All of a sudden, I had time to meet friends and to pursue activities."

One of the things she picked up was rugby. Andrea took it up for recreation but went on to play competitively for several years and even made it to a couple of national try-outs. Sports had always been a big part of her life—her father had been a football player, while her mother had excelled at field hockey, basketball and softball, with golf being her latest pursuit.

Andrea enjoying a few light moments after training a group of yoga teachers.

Stumbling Blocks

Episodes of anxiety and depression had stalked Andrea right from her college days. That was also when she had first taken an interest in yoga. But little did she know that those were early symptoms of a disease that would surface later.

"The thing with bipolar disorder is that you have the genes that may give you the predisposition, and then you have an environment that triggers the genes, like allergic reactions. So, you may have the genes but you may never have the symptoms of bipolar disorder unless something triggers it," Andrea explains.

She weathered it well when her father passed away. "My dad was a World War II veteran. He was an older man. He was fighting cancer for most of my life. I think I was 11 when he had his first heart attack and 14 the second time. As a teenager, I was dealing with the potential death of a parent. So, I had a lot of time to prepare and deal with it. It wasn't easy, but I was at peace with it," she says, fighting back tears.

What became the deal-breaker was her divorce. Andrea was 24 when she got married for the first time. He was a Scotsman she had met during her stint in UK. When the marriage fell apart a few years later, it triggered those rogue genes, bringing her life down around her. "It was a stressful marriage and I did not have the tools to manage it. And when it ended, I could not deal with the emotional upheaval. Anxiety went up and I couldn't handle it."

The illness that had been brewing for a long while went unnoticed by most people around her. "It was the late 1990s, we were all wearing glitter, had coloured hair and going to costume parties. So if you were a little crazy, nobody noticed. But when you break it down into what was really functional, things get hard. I wasn't taking care of myself, I wasn't sleeping. I would talk too much, interrupt people, argue."

All those little habits or quirks that Andrea thought made her unique turned out to be symptoms of bipolar disorder. The situation snowballed—she started having trouble at work, had severe meltdowns, was on the verge of bankruptcy and one day she took all her medication in one shot. It was her friends who saved her, with her ex-husband helping.

"I remember waking up in the hospital and thinking, not so much 'Where am I?' but 'Do I get a break now? Is someone going to help me?' Because I didn't know what was wrong, I didn't know how to stop it. Everything was spinning out of control all the time and I needed a break, I needed help," Andrea says. The diagnosis came as a relief—now she knew what was wrong and there were ways to set it right.

What followed were eight years of putting her life back together and dealing with the debilitating illness. "It was my first time working and being independent without my first husband, financially trying to get back on my feet."

Back to Small Town Living

Andrea wears her emotions on her sleeve and recalling those dark days makes her pause every now and then. It was perhaps the toughest part of her life and there were several missteps before she was on the right track.

"Some people turn to drugs, some people turn to alcohol, some people spend a ton of money. For me, everything manifested in relationships and that was my downfall. I had gotten into another relationship that was not great and I was not healthy enough to be in a relationship. I was in a bad situation and I eventually moved home to Connecticut to start over."

On one hand, that helped—her mother was a great support, as were her sisters. But on the other hand, she had no friends and a terrible job. "I think things went from bad to worse once I left Chicago for Connecticut. Part of it was because I was negative, in a bad place, so I wasn't attracting anyone positive. I don't think I was very likeable—I was sick, I cried a lot, I was very sensitive. I had trouble at work, where people used to make fun of me for the clothes I wore. I was in therapy every single week."

But she had to learn how to get through it. She worked with her doctor to get the medication right and was meticulous with therapy. The one bright spot was that she got herself a dog, which had been trained to be a psychiatric service companion. However, that brought about yet another hurdle—her workplace would not allow the dog to accompany her.

For Andrea, that was the last straw.

"I realised that I needed to get out of there. I knew I needed to get back to where I would be more accepted and of course, a liberal, metropolitan city is a great place for that. It took another year and a half for that to happen, but I started to feel more positive about where I could go." She started reaching out to friends in Chicago, looking for jobs, and as soon as something came up, she was off.

Being the Voice of Bipolar Disorder

One of the first decisions Andrea took when she was back in Chicago was to stop being a victim. She had already come a long way from the last time she was in the city and this time around, she wanted to help. "Having gone through all that I went through, I did not want others to go through it too—being alone, hating yourself, turning people against you. I had to do something to change the perception, to change people's ideas about mental health."

Andrea volunteered with the National Alliance on Mental Illness and became a speaker for the non-profit organisation. She gave lectures at universities for students of psychiatry and psychology on what it was to live with bipolar disorder. She also trained therapists and police officers. She became a regular on the speaking circuit on mental health, even putting in a couple of television appearances.

"I did outreach where people would say my daughter, my sister, or my aunt is suffering, and I would go talk to their family or I would talk to the person. It wasn't always accepted. You can only try. But I felt good about making the effort. It was more than just taking care of myself. It was taking care of other people."

Having always pursued yoga, she now had more reason to put more time into it—yoga has mental health benefits.

That was enough reason for her to get certifications in yoga and she has been teaching it ever since.

Living the Life of Dreams, Finally

The more that Andrea helped people, the better she felt about herself. Healing herself and supporting others worked in building her up to where she was in 2009, when she met her current husband. It changed her life and how she looked at the world. In fact, life then changed rather fast and for the better. In two years, they were married, and within a few months of that, they had moved to Singapore, while also expecting a baby.

It was rugby and common friends that brought them together. "It is the best and healthiest relationship I have ever been in. I think it happened because I put myself in a good mental space to be a good energy out there to attract good energy back."

Now, they are a team. She still has her bad days when even getting out of bed is a struggle, but she has with her a supportive husband who understands bipolar disorder. "It's nice to have a partnership—and not just a marriage—where we support each other. I am living the dream here and he made it possible."

Andrea with her husband
Christopher and her
daughter Georgia.

In Chicago, Andrea had been working two jobs in order to be able to afford her medicines. She was working as a journalist and as a yoga instructor. It was the yoga job that she loved, but had to stay on at the other job to keep paying bills. After the wedding and the subsequent move across the globe, she was gradually able to reduce some stress and that made a world of difference.

Now, she can write for the joy of writing. And that is just what she is doing—she writes on matters close to her heart, which is mental health. "I knew that when I came here I would continue my advocacy work as much as I could. The week I got here, I contacted a girls' home that dealt with mental health, offering to volunteer for them."

Especially in the expat circles, Andrea often observes signs of mental illness. The change of environment triggers symptoms that could spiral out of control. "There is an isolation that comes with this lifestyle, when you are far away from your friends and family. Maybe their partners travel a lot. Then there is the loss of financial independence that several women face when they move here without a job. Sometimes situations come up that people back home don't understand. There are social pressures, relationship pressures; people cheat, people lose money, people make a lot of money and everything changes. These are all triggers and I see it all the time," she says.

For now, Andrea's goals are clear—to get her book published, to continue volunteering in the field of mental health and to make a difference in people's lives. And for herself, to stay in the state of well-being that she now finds herself in. "The goal is to stay in the calmness—*santosha*, or contentment. An even keel, not happy not sad, just right in the middle. Sometimes that's boring. To be excited about things is so much more fun. But it's not healthy and then you don't sleep and you're not eating right. It's better this way."

Dear Ms Expat,

You have to maintain yourself. You are not just a trailing spouse, you are not just a mum, you are not just a partner. You are who you are. You have to do things that build yourself up as an individual so you don't get lost.

Whether it is financial independence or not speaking the language—feeling that you are useless is the worst thing that causes women to give up. Some people say that that's ego. No, it's a sense of self. You have to develop your sense of self, whether you do yoga, have coffee, or join a walking group. If you take care of yourself and if you are relatively content, you can take care of everything else. If you don't take care of yourself, you can't do anything.

No matter how bad things are in your life, you can always rise from the ashes and start again.

Best wishes,
Andrea

Michaela Anchan

New Zealand
Founder, Woolf Works

Creativity Needs Space

When Virginia Woolf inspires you to start a business, you know you've struck gold.

The weekday bustle of the city seems to fall back as one steps into Woolf Works, a co-working space exclusively for women, the only one of its kind in Singapore. The office space is bright and serene, sunlight streaming in through the windows. Two women tap away at laptops while another takes her phone call to the roof terrace.

The space reflects its founder—the soft-spoken Michaela Anchan from New Zealand. The bookshelf right at the entrance holds a couple of much-read copies of Virginia Woolf's *A Room of One's Own*. "The book is what we are named after. She wrote it in the late 1920s. That was almost 100 years ago. But that's exactly true to the reason that I started Woolf Works—that women need to get away. They are so emotionally connected to what is going on in the house, keeping things on schedule and worrying about everyone else. We need to get out of that space to start creating and focus on ourselves professionally. Detach. Having a room of one's own helps to do that," Michaela says.

With two young children, Michaela was quick to spot this need in her own life, while also realising that if she needed it, there would be many others too who would gladly welcome a space to work in. Woolf Works and its growing community of women have given ample proof that she was indeed on the right track.

Before the Beginning

Michaela is no newbie to expat living. It was way back in 2003 that she left her home country. Her first stop was South Korea, where she taught English for a year. She followed it up with a year-long backpacking trip with her sister, covering the Southeast Asian region, China, Tibet and Nepal before winding up in Mumbai, India. In fact, she liked the city so much so that she decided to stay on. It turned out to be an excellent decision, because soon she met her future husband in the city.

"Settling into Mumbai brought a bit of an identity crisis. It took a long time for me to make friends. It was mostly friends from the office or my husband's friends. When I became a mother, I found a mums-and-babies group. It was wonderful to find that support. From there, I found another group where I made lifelong friends—it was a group comprising expat women married to Indians and settled in Mumbai. We shared common stories and were great support to each other."

In the meantime, she also found herself a job and started work with a shipping company. Two years of being in the corporate world gave her a good understanding of the world of business and she decided it was time to take the plunge and start something of her own.

"I set up an e-commerce platform, selling fair trade Indian handicrafts internationally. I was about two months into that, sourcing and working out the business plan when I got pregnant. And then I threw up for the next six months non-stop. Eventually that project got shelved." Soon she found herself turning into a full-time mum, while also pursuing a creative writing degree from a New Zealand university.

It was in 2011 that the idea of Singapore came calling, in the form of a new job opportunity for her husband. Her sister had long been a Singapore resident; in addition to that, the prospects of a better quality of life made the move even more appealing.

As much as she loved Mumbai, there was one aspect that swayed her: "After seven years, I was tired of being the foreigner. There is nothing more I could have done to fully integrate into life there and it got tiring after a while. I thought of my daughter growing up this way, always remaining a little bit of an outsider."

Her daughter was also missing out on the outdoorsy childhood that Michaela had. Having lived just outside of Wellington, Michaela's growing up years had been about biking around with friends, staying out till nightfall, climbing fences, chasing cows, exploring and running wild. Struggling to find a similar experience for her daughter in Mumbai, Singapore came across as an ideal option, being "a neutral ground between New Zealand and India, both geographically and culturally."

Two years after moving to Singapore, during which time she had her second baby, Michaela's urge to get back to pursuing her professional goals was getting the better of her. She started working on her writing only to realise what a struggle it was to work from home. "I found it very hard to switch off from being a mum and being at home and switch on to the work I wanted to get done. I was always being interrupted or distracted. Then I thought, I need my own office where it will be calm and quiet."

Office spaces didn't come cheap. The co-working spaces that she found weren't what she was looking for—they turned out to be mostly tech-oriented, busy and sometimes a bit intimidating.

"I wanted somewhere calm, quiet and beautiful with natural light. Somewhere I can feel inspired to come and work. After talking to other women, I felt that it was quite a common need amongst mums, who were not being productive in a home office, to have somewhere to go to work. I thought maybe this is a project that needed work, maybe I should start my own space." And thus the idea of Woolf Works was born.

The Business of Making Space
Michaela toyed with the idea for a while before actually making the shift from treating it as a hobby to making it

into a business. "I was overwhelmed by how much there was to do and how much there was to put in place. You can make it seem like such a big mountain, you think you couldn't possibly get to the top. But if you just take it step by step, it's not that difficult."

Michaela at the Woolf Works co-working space.

In 2014, Woolf Works opened in Singapore's East Coast and, globally, it was one of only a dozen or so co-working spaces that are exclusively for women. Eventually, it moved to the heart of the city. It was not merely an office space that Michaela built over the span of three years. It was a whole community of women who helped each other and functioned as an excellent professional network. "We have peer circles, lean-in circles, writers' accountability groups. Wherever we can, we form a little peer circle that is helpful to people. I think it has been really great for a lot of women here."

While some women opted for a permanent desk at Woolf Works, others took up flexible plans that had them come in three days a week or just once a week. Soon it was not just mums trying to work in a quiet space, but also other women who wanted to break the monotony of working from home. The first six months were a struggle and it took several events and networking sessions to get the word around.

In three years though, Woolf Works had gained around 150 members and a community of around 1,500 women who associated with it in some way or the other. "I think this is a niche that could see good demand, but there are only 12 or 13 such all-women spaces globally. US and Australia have a few and there are a couple in Japan as well."

In a time when impersonal glass and chrome buildings are the norm for offices, Michaela created a space that had character, that held charm and warmth. "I am not sure where my need for a quiet workplace comes from. I blame it all on Mumbai and motherhood. It made me realise how noise-sensitive I am. It was about having a retreat to escape to."

A space like this is particularly relevant in Singapore, Michaela feels. A lot of women move to Singapore with their husbands' jobs. Many of them use the chance to start a family. A few years later, they struggle with the hurdles of getting back into the corporate world.

"There are a lot of women going through this kind of identity crisis. From the outside, expat life can look fabulous. But I think a lot of women wonder about 'what am I going to do, I feel guilty, when I go back to my home country I am going to have this big gap in my career' and so on. Woolf Works attracts several women who are going through this transition, who need space to figure out what they want to do, maybe set up a business, or just find support."

This is what inspired Catalyst, a 12-week programme run by Woolf Works that helps mothers get back into the workforce. "It is for women who are trying to get back but not sure how. It's about finding some confidence, finding a little bit of excitement and making action plans to move forward. People often get paralysed about what steps to take next. Catalyst helps with that. We bring in mentors and have a peer circle that can be really helpful," Michaela explains.

In the meantime, Michaela's own motherhood experience had changed. "I dropped a lot of the guilt quite early on about not being around for the kids, because when I am not working, I don't think I am a very good mum. I would get frustrated. So, I go with quality over quantity. Now in the time I spend with them, I am happier and fulfilled. I feel better about myself as a role model to my daughter."

Changing Scene, Changing Direction

Three years into this exciting journey, Michaela felt the need to bring a new form to the company. With a sudden mushrooming of co-working spaces in Singapore, the business model needed a revamp. "Co-working economics require a large scale," she says. With scaling up not being an option, Michaela closed down the co-working space and put more focus on the Woolf Works community.

Over the years, Woolf Works had built a strong network of women professionals with peer circles in different interest areas—a support system that hundreds of women in Singapore have come to rely on. Its Catalyst programme attracts great interest from women who are looking at getting back to work after a break. These are aspects of Woolf Works that continue to function, helping women in their professional journeys.

"It has been a huge learning process for me. I was able to recognise what I am good at and what I am not. I learnt the need for processes and delegation," Michaela says. She now intends to use this break to go back to her first love—writing. Having long nourished the dream to write a novel, she is now on the path to see it through.

Dear Ms Expat,

Get out there and get involved in as many communities as possible. See which one works for you—whether it is a book club, a business network, or a parents group. And somewhere you will find a good community that is supportive.

If you are thinking of starting something on your own, get out, meet people and talk about what you want to do. The more you do that, the more you will see that the advantages are twofold. One, you learn how to talk about your business because you see how it lands and you refine your pitch. Secondly, you never know what kind of resources you get connected to. In Singapore especially, it is easy to get connected to a resource—there is always a friend of a friend. If you sit at home and try to work on the idea, you won't move forward.

Best wishes,
Michaela

Dipashree Das

India
Partner Marketing, Netflix

Master of Her Fate,
Captain of Her Soul

"Invictus" reads a tattoo on Dipashree Das's forearm in big, bold letters. A tattoo that she got at a crucial juncture of her life, it represents all that William Ernest Henley's poem by the same title has meant to her: motivation, strength, prayer. It is a hark back to the difficult times, a call to move on, a reminder that she overcame the worst. "I am the master of my fate, I am the captain of my soul," she quotes from the poem; lines that have spurred her on, past every obstacle life threw at her.

Dipashree came to Singapore much the same way as most other expats who move to a new country—with plans and hopes for a wonderful new chapter in life—only to find them crumble around her one by one. But this is not a story of a life unravelling, this is a story of spunk and grit that put that life back together, and how!

She was 11 years old when she decided what she wanted to be professionally and over two decades later, as Partner Marketing for Southeast Asia and India at Netflix, Dipashree says she is well on her way there. She is walking that path with the same determination that brought her this far.

An Influential Childhood

Dipashree grew up in small town Shillong in North East India, with a father who taught her and her younger sister to dream big and a mother who had broken most norms of her times to pursue her career. Even today, she draws generously from her childhood that, looking back, was idyllic and liberal.

"Reading was a big part of growing up. My mother was a Professor of English Literature and retired as the head of her department. That is where my love for literature comes from. I never wanted to study anything else. It was crystal clear in my mind," she reminisces. "My father used to tell us that nothing is impossible and I bought it hook, line and sinker. To me, it's the motto to live by. It has made my life painful, but it has also driven me to an extent I never thought possible."

With these two pillars of strength behind her, leadership qualities came naturally to her at quite a young age. So much so that when the geography teacher went on leave, she took it upon herself to teach the class until she was pulled up and reprimanded: "If you teach the class, what will the teacher teach?" Having faced an audience through stage performances and debates from quite a young age, confidence was never lacking.

It was at that time that Dipashree happened to read about Ted Turner and the setting up of CNN. Impressed by the

Dipashree with her parents Dipok Kumar and Smritirekha, and sister Ananta.

story, she decided that the media industry was where she wanted to be. "I knew then that this was who I want to be—I want to be what he was for television. I told myself at 11 years of age, that by the time I am 40, I will be the CEO of a very big media company," she says. And with her current job, she could be headed in the right direction. "This is the job that, it's safe to say, anyone who has anything to do with content and entertainment would want to be a part of. I feel that it could actually make my dream happen."

Out in the Big, Bad World

Armed with her love for literature and a rock solid ambition, Dipashree left her hometown at the age of 18 to pursue higher studies in Delhi. "My three years at Lady Shri Ram College for Women were watershed years. It changed me as a person. I was never shy, but I always felt that maybe I am lesser because I come from a small town. It is the underdog mentality. I think it keeps you grounded and prevents you from becoming arrogant."

Having kept herself busy with not just academics but also debate competitions, academic forums and the student union, she feels those years were crucial in defining her professional ethics and how she would function. "I have nothing against hard work. I can work myself to death and I will not question it."

Right out of college, she was recruited by Unilever, where she spent a few difficult but fruitful years learning the ropes while "selling soap". The going was tough from the word go. Not only was she the youngest, she was among the very few without an MBA degree.

"My first role after the management trainee period was leading a sales team of 45 people who were all in the age range of 30-45. I was 21. It was a huge mistake, if you ask me," she recalls. But what started out as a disaster soon turned around thanks to sheer hard work. "The first two years were living hell. But it made me very tough—it now takes a lot to intimidate me."

Dipashree went on to have a few good years at the company. It was also here that she met her future husband. After five years of having known each other, they tied the knot at a dream ceremony that Dipashree planned—a sunset wedding on the beaches of Goa.

It was just before the wedding that she made a career shift and moved to broadcast media, joining one of

India's largest television news networks, New Delhi Television (NDTV). It was a time of excitement—she was on track, finally in the space that she had always wanted to be in.

"I was so excited, like a child in a candy shop. This was what I wanted to do. I started off as a business correspondent, doing features, interviews and documentaries. Then I moved on to doing branded content."

A year later though, things weren't as rosy. At work, much anticipated promotions weren't coming along despite meeting her targets, while at home, her husband was moving to Singapore for work.

After a few months of trying to make the long-distance relationship work, Dipashree decided to prioritise the marriage over her career and moved to Singapore. "I remember my father asking me, are you absolutely sure about this decision, because your career is a very important part of who you are."

When Life Unravels

Almost immediately after her move, one by one the pieces began to fall apart.

On the very first day, Dipashree realised that she was going to be pretty much on her own, whether it was to find the closest supermarket or to get herself a job. Her husband was almost always travelling abroad for work and she had no friends in the city.

On the work front, she was exploring setting up a bureau for NDTV, but despite giving it an earnest try, that didn't seem feasible. Also, her talks with another major financial company for a job fell through. This falling out at a rather advanced stage came as a big blow.

She started a job hunt, sending out applications and making cold calls. After several weeks of it, she finally had a call for an interview and eventually joined a production house, Oak3 Films. "The woman who runs that agency, my first boss in Singapore, is still one of the most inspiring women I have ever met. I cannot be more thankful to her for giving me that break because no one else was. For me, it was a break in a new market during a bad recessionary phase."

But just when she was about to join, her father had a stroke. It was a difficult period in every way, what with travelling regularly to India to take care of her father and managing a new job. Nevertheless, in a few months she had settled well into the job, doing a lot of TV content. Before long she was hired by Channel NewsAsia and was soon leading its digital team.

Things, though, weren't looking great on the personal front—the couple were headed towards a divorce. For Dipashree, it was as sudden as it was unexpected and it left her devastated. "I remember it like it was yesterday, how I was lying on the balcony and crying my eyes out. I had been a unit with him from when I was 21. It was like having the rug pulled from under my feet."

What followed were several months of emotional trauma and self-doubt. "But inside me, I think a switch had flipped. I felt like I was pretending; like I was an imposter living in that house," Dipashree recalls. "Except my sister, no one knew what was going on— not my parents, not my closest friends. I didn't want to talk about it."

Eventually, after a long drawn out process, Dipashree was on her own. "I went from living in one of the most expensive condos in Singapore to living out of a suitcase in several of my friends' homes."

A divorce is difficult as it is. When it happens in a country miles away from home and loved ones, it is doubly so. Moreover, it changed her as a person. "It took me a long time to trust someone again. But there is a positive too. I was always self-reliant, but I did not know how much more I had to step up until this happened. Now I am super self-reliant."

Given the circumstances and her yearning to be with her family, she did consider returning to India. "I even found a job there. But suddenly I said to myself, why should I go back?" It was now time to reclaim her life.

Putting the Pieces Back

Determined to reach her goals, Dipashree dug her heels in. She moved out of her friend's apartment to a shared accommodation, which was all she could afford on her modest pay. What she had in plenty by now were friends. "I would wake up on Sundays and not know what to do with my life. Two things saved me—my job and how much I loved it, and my friends," she says.

She started looking for better job opportunities and soon moved to Singtel. It marked a new phase in her life. For one, it came with better pay, which meant she could move into her own apartment. The job had its ups and downs, but she did well enough to win four Chief Commercial Officer awards during her stint there.

"It was a golden run. I had more money, I started travelling by myself. I went to Australia by myself and was in Sydney on New Year's Eve, hanging out with complete strangers. I learnt what it was like to focus on myself," she says.

Since then, things only got better, both with her job as well as her healing process.

But that was when another blow came, with the death of her father. "I am not a very religious person. I think of god as an energy. Now I have a form to it, I see him as my dad," she says.

Present Perfect

Dipashree couldn't possibly be more thrilled about her career than she is now. She finds it to be the right confluence of content, technology and brand building.

"I am absolutely delighted with where I am right now professionally. I have received so much positive feedback

Dipashree at her current work place.

in the last few months that I feel I really can crack it. I have to thank the breakdown of my marriage to have pushed me the way it did. Personally, I still have a lot of stuff to figure out—how not to bring the baggage from my last relationship into the new one, coping with losing my father—it's a work in progress. My mother, sister, boyfriend and friends are my pillars of strength."

Her vision board for when she is 40 has her featured on magazine covers as a business woman to be reckoned with. As she grows in her career, so does her belief that every step ahead for her is a step ahead for other women too.

"Had it not been for my late maternal grandma, who was uneducated, insisting that her four daughters get master's degrees, had it not been for my mother who went on to become the head of her department in a day and age when women were not doing half of that, I wouldn't be here. If my women bosses hadn't believed in me like no man ever has, I wouldn't be here. Because you are there, someone else can aspire to be there."

Dear Ms Expat,

Never back down. Coco Chanel said there is no problem in life that you can't conquer; put on some red lipstick, put on some high heels and do your thing, whatever that is. Whether it is going to yet another interview where you will be turned down, or facing up to that boss you don't like.

I think what helped me and can help a lot of others is having clarity of where you want to be. Even if you have zero clarity on the route you want to take, focus on the goal. Work towards that with humility and dedication.

If you have done something meaningful, please help other people. If you want more women out there, what is your role? Who are you bringing to the boardroom with you? Don't stand against women, stand with them.

Best wishes,
Dipashree

Manale Ganiere

Switzerland

Founder & Director, Renascentia Pte Ltd

Rebirth in More Ways Than One

When adventure takes you places, when new milestones in life leave you gasping, what do you do? You pause, take a deep breath and adapt. You reinvent yourself to fit into the new circumstances. You put yourself through a rebirth and emerge with a fresh, new life.

Or at least, that is what Manale Ganiere did. More than once, at that. The first time was when she moved half way across the globe and was immediately met with unexpected challenges. Then again, when motherhood revealed to her aspects of her own nature that she had been unaware of. And yet another time, when she turned into an entrepreneur, stepping into a zone that was new, scary and exciting all at once.

Animated and positively radiating energy, Manale is a

lawyer from Switzerland who made Singapore her home five years ago. Born to a Swiss father and Lebanese mother, she comes with an equal measure of the exuberance of her mother's family and the quiet calm of her father's. Having had a Lebanese upbringing in the heart of Europe, Manale pegs herself as an international citizen rather than an expatriate.

It was a sense of adventure, a desire to do something crazy and a life goal of working abroad for a while that brought Manale and her husband here. Now, Manale runs her own company, Renascentia, which offers cross-border consultation for Swiss companies setting up business in Singapore and vice versa.

Grabbing the Right Opportunity

"I was working at a highly reputable law firm in Switzerland, and there was a possibility of me becoming junior partner soon. But I decided against it." It would have been a dream opportunity for most others in her position. But Manale saw it as a job that would keep her tied down for several years.

"I wasn't even 30 years old and I couldn't picture myself in that life for the next 30 years! My husband and I

decided that it was time to go and do something crazy."
In taking that decision, she had opened a door towards
new prospects.

"As a Swiss-qualified lawyer, I couldn't practice law
anywhere else. Switzerland is under civil law jurisdiction
while countries like the UK, Singapore and the U.S.
come under common law jurisdiction. So, if I had to
give up being a lawyer, I didn't want to do that and go
to London or Spain and be just one hour away from
Switzerland. It had to be something bigger. That's when
Asia came up."

Her family was left puzzled; they wondered why two
people would put themselves through uncertainties like
these. But Manale counts it as the best decision they
ever took.

Their stay in Singapore began with no jobs, little money
and tourist visas in hand. The visa allowed them to stay for
three months and they put a minimum-risk plan in place.
If one of them got a job in three months, they would stay
on for another three months. But after half a year, if the
other person still could not find an opportunity, they
would go back.

"There was no risk. I wouldn't become someone less competent in six months; I could still go back home and find a job. But I couldn't leave without trying."

Her husband, being in the cybercrime industry, found a job in a week's time. "It was not an expatriate package, but a local job with local salary. He decided to take it because that would enable us to get an apartment, an employment pass, have a bank account and not be tourists anymore."

And thanks to some contacts, soon she too had a part-time job at a Swiss company. "Since it was a Swiss company, I was still working with Swiss law. I took it up on a part-time basis so that I could get experience and expertise in the trust industry with common law. I was studying and working at the same time, which was great."

With that first job, she learnt everything there was to know about setting up a company in Singapore and managing it, something that became crucial to what she would eventually do.

A few years in, Manale was working long hours at a new job, while also completing her studies. "I just loved it, it was really interesting. It was hard, I had to work from Monday to Sunday. I used to study from 6 to 9 in the morning and then be at work from 9 to 8 in the evening. It was crazy for two years." Her company also required her to set up a new office in Dubai, with the objective that she would eventually become the director of that facility.

That was when she got pregnant. "I did manage to set up the office before I went on maternity leave. I worked until about five days before delivering. I loved every moment of it. I loved being pregnant and working at the same time. In fact, I was travelling till the seventh month."

There were low points too. With all her friends in faraway Switzerland, Manale was lonely in the new country. And given the long hours she was working, there had been no time to make new friends. Of course, she had an amazing professional network, but very few that she could call a confidante.

"I didn't have any friends here that I could share my pregnancy stories with. In a way, it was good because rather than worry about all the questions in my head, I told myself that as long as I am happy, the baby is happy."

Motherhood Brings an Identity Crisis

When the baby came along, life changed completely. "I think I had a huge identity crisis. Once I became a mother, I was no longer the person I was, or who I thought I was," she remembers. The delivery was followed by some complications, on the whole leaving her with a fresh perspective on how she wanted to live from that moment on.

"I just wanted to be a mum. That was a huge defining moment in my life because I had never imagined myself to be the kind of person who wanted to be nothing else but a doting mum. I did not want to go back to work, all I wanted was to be with my baby," Manale says, throwing her hands in the air.

That strong sense of motherhood was probably already in her Lebanese genes. "Lebanese people are very family-oriented and I had suddenly become one of them! Everything that I was pushing away, I became."

When Swiss Meets Lebanese

Manale's mother has been a strong influence in her life. As a young woman, her mother had had to flee Lebanon in the midst of a war, leaving behind a life of financial and social independence. An osteopath by profession, she had built her life in Switzerland from scratch.

"My mother is my model. She is fearless, tough and resilient. She is tiny but she has this energy that is all-pervading. She worked Monday to Sunday and helped thousands of people heal. At the same time, she is also very humble and does a lot of charity work."

Though born in Switzerland, Manale was brought up as Lebanese, amidst a large Arabic-speaking family and generous meals. She thinks of her father as a gentle bear, whose happiness came from having his family around, the calm core of their home in Lausanne.

Since childhood, Manale and her two younger siblings had realised that they were different from other families around them. "We never ate Swiss food, it was Lebanese all the time. We were always surrounded by craziness. The door was always open for family and friends and at every meal, there would be about 15 people at the table. There was food all the time—you feel sad, eat; you feel happy, eat; you feel overwhelmed, eat. It was about being together, there would be 10 different conversations going on at the same time. It was chaotic and colourful," she exclaims, nearly out of breath with that peppy description.

"I realised only after becoming a mother myself that being Lebanese is central to my identity and who I am."

Being married to a Swiss, Manale now hopes that their daughter has the best of both worlds—the carefree chaos of the Lebanese as well as the calmness and discipline of the Swiss. They want her to learn Arabic and enjoy the Arab cuisine, but they value their private time as a family too.

"We are bringing up a blonde girl in Singapore. She has started preschool and speaks English and French. When my mum visits, she speaks Arabic with her. Even though English is not our mother tongue, we end up speaking to her in English because we are surrounded by English-speaking people. She doesn't even know she speaks three languages. She is not even two and a half years old and that's her normality. That's what living abroad is about. It's about being open, learning from different cultures."

The Birth of Renascentia

When Manale went back to work after her maternity leave, she found she had changed so much that she did not enjoy her work anymore. At the end of two months, she had left the job. It was as much a shock for her as it was for those who knew her to be a driven and strong woman who loved her work, whose profession formed such a large part of her identity.

Motherhood had changed Manale's priorities. The impending move to Dubai did not seem rosy anymore, even though she had family there and she would be closer home.

"So I quit. I just wanted to be a mum for a while. I knew I couldn't stay at home forever. That's not who I am. But at that moment, I just wanted to spend time with my little one and not think about my career. Those were the best two months of my life," Manale says.

It was towards the end of this break that an opportunity came her way. A Swiss company was setting up business in Singapore and had contacted her for legal help. With that as the first client, Manale decided to set up her own cross-border consultancy firm, Renascentia.

Renascentia is Latin for "rebirth". Even though her friends and family discouraged her from going with it as the name for her company ("It's unpronounceable, it's not good branding."), she stuck to it because the word meant a lot to her.

"Rebirth is what I went through after becoming a mother, in more ways than one. And that is also what you do when you cross borders and set up a home abroad. It is a rebirth for your company as well because you have to start all over again within a new jurisdiction, a new culture."

To Manale, rebirth was part of her own story. From her mother's history of leaving a war-torn nation to her own move to Singapore, starting from scratch is a concept she understands well. "When you do it, you build resilience, you build knowledge, you build experiences. That's what I did all my life."

For this new chapter of her professional life, her husband had one bit of valuable advice: "It doesn't matter if you are a success, it doesn't matter if you fail, but enjoy the process." Though initially that did not seem like much, Manale soon found the wisdom in it.

"Being on your own is challenging, it's hard work, a struggle. As a lawyer, I was good at organising, managing

Manale's Singapore experience has made her push boundaries.

a team and taking care of all the required legal aspects. But here I was as an entrepreneur and I had no idea how to go about it. I had to redefine and relearn all the skills. I am the accountant, the business developer, the lawyer and the web designer. I am struggling, but it is the best time of my life. Now I know what it is to enjoy the process."

Having started the company, there was much that she had to figure out, starting with the branding and marketing of her company to managing the legalities for her client's business. She joined a business incubator programme to hone her skills and it turned out to be a crucial phase in Manale's life.

It gave her many learning experiences and helped with her fledgling business. While earlier she was unsure about getting out there and testing the waters, she is now more confident. "I have my pitch, I have my clients, I know what problem I solve and I know how to solve it," she says.

International Citizen vs Expat

Singapore is not Manale's first international experience. Her studies and work saw her living in Syria, Dubai, Canada, Austria and Germany at various points in life; she speaks French, German, English and Arabic. That leads her to consider herself more of an international citizen rather than an expat. "I cannot consider myself an expat. For me, expat seems to have a feel of not having a choice— like when your company sends you abroad, or when you are following a spouse. It has a sense of obligation."

To her, being international is about creating a home abroad; it is not merely a place you are passing through. "That's who I am; it's being international. That's why I do what I do as a corporate lawyer—I help entrepreneurs cross borders to create a home abroad for their businesses. It is not just about tax and legality. You are going to start over in a new place, you are sending over your employees. It is about culture, lifestyle, language and so many other aspects."

Whether you call it being international or being an expat, moving abroad changes you. "It teaches you how to be flexible, less judgmental and more open-minded. In that sense, it's inspiring. But you have to be willing to try, even if it is a struggle."

For Manale, the last few years have been an experience that has made her push her boundaries, find herself and cement her priorities.

"Back home, I have my friends, my work and other routine exercises. Why would I take myself out of my comfort zone and try something new? But when you are abroad in an unknown environment, you don't have those pillars holding you up. You have to look for opportunities. When you are open to explore and discover, things begin to unfold. At one point, you will start connecting the dots and everything will make sense."

Manale with her husband Simon.

Dear Ms Expat,

From my experience, I realised that it is all about having the right mindset—be flexible, be open, have fun. Whatever be the reason that has made you an expat, enjoy the experience. Be willing to take chances, be willing to go out of your comfort zone.

It is going to be difficult. You are going to feel alone, misunderstood, nostalgic. That is normal and that is alright because it is in those moments that your mind opens to new possibilities—grab them.

Best wishes,
Manale

Victoria Mintey

United Kingdom

Actor and Founder, Wag the Dog

When the Actor Takes the Stage

The stage is lit with pink, blue and red lights, depicting the myriad emotions that characters bring in with their words and actions. The sky turns a bright shade of orange, adding its own bit of drama. Fort Canning is dressed up for the year's first show of Shakespeare in the Park, to witness the classic love story of *Romeo and Juliet*.

Victoria Mintey waits in the wings for her cue. She looks at the audience—picnic mats and foldable chairs have been laid out. The balmy weather of Singapore cools down as evening sets in, a light breeze bringing with it the smell of freshly cut grass. The heady rush that precedes the first scene takes her back to her stage performances as a child in Northern Ireland and the many parts she has played ever since.

It is all rather surreal for Victoria to be standing here as part of the cast of this grand production—after having put in years of struggle in the bard's own country, it is here on this tropical island that she has come into her own.

Victoria has theatre coursing through her veins and it is the force that has driven her through the difficult years. Her days as an actor in London started with a host of temporary jobs to help pay her bills, peppered with long audition queues and doing roles in the vibrant fringe theatre scene.

Today, with the same ease with which she juggles different characters, Victoria plays multiple roles in her professional life—she is not only an actor, but also a corporate trainer, voice-over artist and founder of the theatre group Wag the Dog.

The Opening Act

In her home town near Belfast, patrolling army men in camouflaged outfits were the norm. The young students in a school next door to the army cantonment were unaware of the political tsunami that had swept through the region a decade earlier. The violence of the Northern

Ireland conflict meant that cars were always scanned for bombs and bags checked at malls—it was all a part of life.

The eldest daughter of high-school teachers, Victoria was an ideal student—never pulled up for unfinished homework or bad grades. An introvert, she pushed her younger sister ahead to make first introductions with new people, only inching in after the ice was broken.

But on stage, Victoria transformed.

"I fell in love with theatre and acting when I was just five. I am sure I had nerves, but I don't remember them." She recalls playing a part and owning it every single time— the characters, the space, the people in the show and the experience.

"It was the most fun I ever had, doing two crazy intense weeks of rehearsal and then going on to do two or more performances. You have a common goal. Everyone is working towards putting this play up and everyone has a character. You learn your dance moves, your notes. That is when I realised that I can get up on stage and do anything."

By the age of seven, Victoria was learning the piano and violin. "My mum is very musical. When she was teaching in the primary school I went to, she would do a complete musical every year—say *Oliver!*, *Annie* or *Joseph and the Amazing Technicolor Dreamcoat.*"

Victoria's early experience in performing arts and exposure to musical instruments made her realise that singing was her first love. She started vocal lessons when she was around 15. "I initially started with classical singing and then went on to study musical theatre singing. That was the ultimate dream! I got to go to classes and sing songs from musicals all the time. I got the highest grade in that." Her eyes light up at the memory.

Soon enough, it was time to play on a larger stage. Victoria moved to college in Durham University in the north of England.

"I chose my university because I knew it had a really strong theatre scene. All my spare time was spent rehearsing for shows. Students were directing, choreographing, producing and acting. We had some fantastic older students who would be the musical directors and they were excellent at coaching me. They had some really cool facilities there as well, including a little crumbly old theatre that we could use anytime of the year."

While her love for theatre helped choose a college, Victoria was still indecisive about what she wanted to pursue as a career in the long term. She decided to do a science degree, and mixed and matched subjects to find out where her interest lay.

At the end of three years, she had graduated with specialisation in anthropology and psychology, but decided to pursue theatre. "I think it was always there, but I didn't admit it to myself. I always wanted to perform, I wanted to be on stage." Being a straight A student, choosing a profession that brought with it a fair share of struggles and low pay didn't dampen Victoria's spirits.

"My parents are incredibly supportive and always have been. Otherwise I wouldn't be here now. They lent me money to try and get into drama school. In retrospect, I realise how great that was! And all that was done in a fairly understated way. It wasn't even like they were trying to win Parents of the Year Award. I am very lucky that even though they had no experience of it, they didn't stop me," she laughs.

And that is when things got dirty, dusty, sweaty, tiring and great!

"Getting into drama school for the 12-month course was intensive. Some people say that in drama school they totally beat you down and put you back together again. Although that didn't quite happen to me, it made me doubt myself a lot, because every day they make you do something that you may not be good at. It was frustrating for me because I am used to knowing stuff and being smart."

It was a tough and interesting year, which wasn't all sunshine and rainbows and doing pirouettes. It ended with her class of 20 being well-prepared for acting work, but not well-equipped in the ways of getting acting jobs. "They teach you what to do after you get the jobs. I know that when I walk into a rehearsal room, I need to do my warm up and take notes from the director. I know how to portray a character inside out. But how do I actually get there? When I graduated from London, I didn't have a clue what to do."

What followed were four tough years in London trying to break into an industry that was oversubscribed by about tenfold. "I showed up for jobs that didn't even pay anything and there were 400 people in the queue!"

Being a tiny, tiny fish in the massive ocean resulted in Victoria managing few roles, being a part of the fringe theatre scene and spending most of her time on part-time jobs that allowed her the flexibility to audition on short notice. "This was the bit that really frustrated me. I knew there were these smart jobs I could have done, but there I was answering phones or waitressing, to pay rent—jobs I could do in my sleep. I knew I was better than this."

Fortunately for her, the ordeal ended. She got a job on a cruise ship for a year and her world changed overnight.

Sailing into a New Life

Victoria's life on the cruise began with training in America with the rest of the team, all from a range of nationalities and across different age groups. As lead singer, she got to sing and perform all the belting, impressive numbers. "I embraced everything. The money was good as I didn't have to pay any taxes. It was also very fulfilling as a singer, although not so much as an actor."

The highlight though, was the travel. "We started off

in the Mediterranean, spending three months cruising around the region. I visited Venice, Florence, Rome, Athens, Egypt, saw the pyramids. It was an exceptional experience and the job was fairly easy as we worked only in the evenings, when the ship set sail."

As her professional life picked up, her personal life also went into warm, unchartered territories. Victoria had met someone just eight weeks before she left. "I was wondering what's going to happen, since I was going to be away for over 12 months. But we continued speaking over Skype, having some awkward conversations." She realised it was the "real thing" when he visited her on the ship after five months of her being on board. "I was really happy when he came to see me. We were in Italy then. I think that's when we realised we were in love."

From Europe, the cruise went to Asia, docking in Thailand, Singapore and China through many months. "My boyfriend visited me again during my birthday. We had a great experience, riding elephants, getting four-dollar massages and being off the ship for 12 hours. I was heartbroken when he went back and I knew then I didn't want to do this any longer."

This, coupled with a highly-regimented life on the cruise, made Victoria give up her plans to do another few years of cruise life. She headed back to London and a secure relationship.

The theatre scene however still hadn't picked up for Victoria. "I had not got a West End production and I wasn't on the conveyor belt for jobs. My agent wasn't great and I wasn't getting many auditions." And this seemed to serve as a catalyst in Victoria's decision to move to Singapore with her boyfriend when he got an offer from his company.

"I hadn't even tried Ireland for theatre, because I didn't want to be too far away from London, where the action really is. But when Singapore came in I decided to take the plunge as I didn't have much to lose."

A Fresh Start under the Arc Lights

The Singapore theatre scene brought new opportunities for Victoria. "The first year was like the London days, with me trying to get auditions and even working for free. Then I got a kids' show with the Singapore Repertory Theatre and things started to look up." She went on to be offered a role in Shakespeare in the Park. Since then, Victoria has

Victoria on stage for *The 39 Steps*.

done children's musicals, several plays and multiple voice-overs for brands like British Airways. She also got an opportunity to dabble in TV, playing a nun in *Mata Mata*.

She believes her best role to date has been in the theatre production *The 39 Steps*. "It was fantastically written and I played three parts in it—a German femme fatale who gets stabbed, a ditzy blond and a shy Scottish lady who lives with her abusive husband up on the hills."

Having had the opportunities to explore various roles and mediums, Victoria slips into comparing her experiences in the London and Singapore theatre scenes. She believes that there is immense openness of information sharing in Singapore. "In London, audition details were rarely shared. But in Singapore, almost all the jobs I get here are from someone mentioning my name. You don't run into many actors and the few that we run into stay in our minds. Also, maybe because there is lower competition—good actors are noticed."

The other difference has been more personal for Victoria. "I think I have grown along the way. I have become more positive and although this may sound like a cliché, I give 100 percent to every role I get. In that sense, any time I get any part, it is fulfilling because I work hard to make it good."

She is also happy biding her time for good jobs to come through. "Some people get disappointed after setting big goals and dreams. But at the same time if you expect too much too soon, it is easier to get deflated. I went about trying to pick up whatever experiences and contacts I could. People get off the boat every day here—I'm not the first and I won't be the last."

The Business of Art

So far Victoria has watched the show from the sidelines. She now believes that the time is ripe to take centre stage and create new opportunities for actors and theatre artists.

"I have created my own theatre group called Wag the Dog. We call it that because actors usually are at the bottom of the food chain and we want to reverse the trend. What normally happens is that the director and producer come up with the idea, book a large theatre, plan the audience and then reach out to the actors. This leaves the actors with very little choice in what role, type of play and money they are most likely to make. We plan to go in differently—we are a group of actors with the story and we plan to fund it a little by ourselves. We will then book a place to do it and finally get the people in to see it. So, we are the tail wagging the dog."

The theatre group has seven people—one director and six actors, a combination of expats and locals. "There's definitely going to be a steep learning curve. We initially started off with just three people, but then auditioned to get more people in. It is a very slow burn but I'm happy it will happen."

And it's not just a theatre group that Victoria has founded, she has also single-handedly set up a successful corporate training venture. "This started with an invitation to role play for a big training day. Someone needed actors to play customer and shareholders. It was for Shell Oil Company

Victoria with the cast of *Jack and the Beanstalk*.

and I had to play a character showing her displeasure at the digging up of a nature reserve for the next refinery. It was an improvised role helping the participants to practice their communications skills. I was super nervous, but it was an amazing feeling—to apply my acting work into real world situations."

Starting off there, Victoria now works with corporates, training their teams on presentations skills, interpersonal communications and rapport building. "This business is growing for me each week and I find it immensely rewarding to help people build confidence in their communication style."

Victoria's life in Singapore has been a transforming journey on both personal and professional levels. From getting married to starting and growing businesses, Victoria's six years in the country have been momentous and she continues to confront and manage various challenges. "As an actor, I don't focus on the long term much, it has always been very point-to-point, but now I am working on planning for the future, especially drawing out the plan for the corporate training business. It is also a challenge to learn the art of negotiating here. The acting profession doesn't pay much. I know I create immense value and I am learning how to convey that message."

Back in London, when Victoria was still struggling to find her place in the theatre world and surviving a mundane job, she had made a promise to herself. "If I still didn't get anything decent by the time I turned 30, I would change directions in life and give up this pursuit." Singapore with its roller-coaster emotional and professional ride has helped her keep her passion alive. "This could not have happened anywhere else. And I have honoured the promise I made to myself."

Dear Ms Expat,

Wear your heart on your sleeve to allow people to meet the real you and understand how they can support you and you them. Singapore is a place where people will offer help, advice, company, connections, coffee—join in this spirit of sharing right away; you are never the newest kid in town.

Friends, truly great friends, will come into your life here and one day they will go. Don't be discouraged, continue to meet new people and invest in these friendships no matter how many times you have to say goodbye.

Best wishes,
Victoria

Christine Edwards

Australia

Founder, Honeycombers

The Business of
Knowing Singapore

In the small Australian town of Moree in New South
Wales, there was a little shop called The Gift Barrel
where women of the neighbourhood co-operative sold
handicraft products. Sharing space with these were
ribbon hairbands sold by Christine Edwards, her very
first business venture. All of 12 years of age, she had
spotted an opportunity and created hair accessories to
meet the demand among young girls like her.

Enterprising, innovative and resourceful—that's Chris
for you.

"I caught the entrepreneurial bug really early. I always
knew I wanted to start something on my own,"
says Chris, now Founder of Honeycombers, one of
Singapore's leading lifestyle platforms. A go-to website

to stay updated about all that's happening in and around Singapore, Honeycombers has now branched out to Bali and Jakarta and is poised to launch in Hong Kong as well.

It was over a decade ago that Chris moved to Singapore with four boxes and no job. Now, Chris's home has three kids and her website gets over half a million unique visitors a month. "I have enjoyed creating my business. I think if I hadn't enjoyed it, I wouldn't do it. I have also worked very hard and put in long hours. I was motivated because I was doing it for myself. That is very rewarding."

An Independent Childhood

The Honeycombers office is done up in bright orange shades. Product samples lie around, blending in with the bustle and calm. Chris's workspace resonates with vibes of her honest, cheerful and confident self.

She draws much of her can-do attitude from her childhood. "I was brought up on a massive 24,000-acre property in Moree. My childhood was very different; the urbanness of today's lives was not there. Now kids need to be taught how to ride a bike, but for us all that just happened along the way. We were on the farm, we rode horses, bikes. It was very different and very beautiful."

It was a whole lot independent too. Chris was just five years old when she started a daily commute of four hours to school and back. To cut down this commute, she started boarding school at the age of 11. She completed her university and picked up her first job in Sydney. Life had settled into quiet normalcy, as marriage and home ownership followed in quick succession.

On the professional front, Chris had a senior role at Krispy Kreme as their marketing director for Australia. "It was their first franchise market outside of the U.S. We worked on establishing the brand presence across the region, reaching out to everyone through PR. But while the role was exciting, I didn't feel adequately challenged."

Reason enough why she didn't think twice when her husband got an opportunity to move out of Australia. "My husband's company said that he could move to Singapore, as there was a job for him there. I quit my job, packed up our lives and came here."

Apprehensions about her move followed her along. "I

remember calling my mum and saying, 'Oh my God! Have I taken the right decision?'"

Creating a Publishing Brand

It would have been safe to assume that as a senior marketing professional, landing a role in Singapore would be easy. Unfortunately, that is not how it played out. "I remember having conversations with recruiters and being told that it would be tough to find a job at my salary level. I was asked to consider a salary drop of around 60-70 percent. At that point, you start asking questions like, what am I really worth!"

Keeping the pedal to the metal, Chris networked a lot in the early days. "The company that relocated us hosted a morning tea and helped us meet people here. I remember going for catch-ups with mums and talking about school schedules and the like, even when I had no kids of my own," she laughs.

Chris finally struck gold when she saw a job ad looking for a self-starter and passionate individual for a role. The only catch—it was in publishing! "I had never done publishing in my life. But I read the ad and I told my husband—that's me!"

Chris with her husband Jason and children Evie, Louis and Darcy.

Thankfully for her, the American recruiters thought the same and after just two interviews, Chris started her professional life in Singapore with Asia City Publishing as general manager. "Adjusting to the new work culture was interesting. The training for this role was in Hong Kong and I remember landing there on the first day of work at 9 a.m. I was shocked to find the office closed! People walked in at 10 a.m. In Australia, 8:30 a.m. is late."

Office schedules weren't the only thing that had her stumped. "I had no cross-cultural experience and I was leading a group of 10 local employees. They saw me as a foreigner with no publishing experience at all. It was a fairly stressful time. My husband constantly asked me to quit."

In retrospect, Chris sees these as stepping stones for her to set up her own publishing business. After her stint with Asia City Publishing, she worked with some friends on an online publishing platform as commercial partner for a year. "It was funny! All this work was so different from what I had done. Earlier I had no idea how to run a business or set up a content publishing platform."

With all this relevant experience under her belt, Chris set up Honeycombers.

"I saw this trend in the U.S. where people were subscribing in droves to content sites that provided an insider's guide to living in each city. We saw one that focussed on 'what to do in New York' and realised that was what Singapore needed! That's how Honeycombers came about."

Singapore now is very different from what it was almost a decade back. "I recall writing an article—'6 places in Singapore to have espresso coffee'. That piece took some extensive research. Now, there must be about 60 good places!"

On the Growth Path

Picture this. A multitasking Chris, building her website, researching and writing for Honeycombers, while with one foot she gently rocks her baby's bouncer.

That's pretty much how she worked on the brand. She set up the business in December 2008 and eight months later, had her first baby. "Initially, I worked out of a home office. But with a kid, things moved to the dining table! I worked from home for 2–3 years. I enjoyed writing while bringing up my baby. I had my husband edit all the articles I wrote." During that time, her husband also chose to work during the night since his job gave him that flexibility. This came as some much-needed support for Chris during her working hours.

As work built up, Chris hired a couple of freelance writers, because sometimes she needed more content than she could produce.

Motherhood only strengthened her resolve to work harder and build something for her kids. "It is interesting.

Motherhood made me want to pursue a career even more strongly. Since I was the boss and worked from home, I had a very flexible work place. Most of my work would be done through naps or when my helper would take my children to the park. I would set myself goals. Give myself 40 minutes and then go back to feeding or spending time with the kids."

The trigger for scaling up the business came when one of the freelancers told her that she had to pick up a full-time role and wouldn't be able to freelance anymore. "I remember saying that I can't imagine she won't be writing for me anymore. She was really good. And that's when it struck me—I could offer her a full-time role!"

And that's how Honeycombers got its first employee in 2012. And Chris got an office space a year later. Since then, the company has been growing from strength to strength and now has 40 employees. Chris initially started Honeycombers as a boutique content business and saw her original audience to be just expats. But that has now expanded to include locals as well. "When we do reader surveys, it comes back with more locals than expats, which is wonderful. It is an interesting insight for all of us. We have also been lucky really, because we never called ourselves the expat guide. And that comes from my background in marketing. Why wouldn't you be for everyone? I think that was a great place to start."

Honeycombers now has two more online properties. From being a popular site for expert recommendations and restaurant reviews, it now provides a content marketing platform for clients to tell their stories. "Advertising through editorialised content is a very powerful way to market to an audience." While initially only expat businesses had shown interest, it now includes local businesses, SMEs, MNCs and even the Singapore government. "I tell my team often that we do have the best job in the world!"

Singapore has had a big role to play in helping Chris achieve success in her business. "This is a land of opportunities. When you are an expat and you are coming into a country that is changing so rapidly, you get to see the opportunities a lot more clearly. It is very interesting because it makes you think about what you can bring to Singapore that it doesn't have yet at this moment. I am very glad that we made the move and I am also very happy that I struggled. I believe that sometimes the best things come out of the worst situations."

While the country helped her to create a thriving business, Chris believes it also ensured that her kids are well-adjusted and more culturally aware. A mother of three, she believes the world has become a bigger space for them since she moved here, in more ways than one. "It is the only place in the world where a person who knows only one language can participate in so many different cultural experiences. This is what I love about Singapore. All my children were born here and they see the world very differently from the way we saw it. In fact, I don't think our kids see the cultures like we do, they think it is very normal that everyone is very different."

A Step Back, a Step Ahead

Having been at the helm for so many years, Chris has now dialled it down a notch to spend time with her children. She has hired a managing director to handle day-to-day operations. In the last few months, she has been putting in about 10 hours a week, giving more time to the family. "I think that as an entrepreneur, that is the flexibility you have."

Although starting up and putting the business in place has been tough, Chris believes that the years blur out when you are having fun. Way back, when she was still contemplating heading out on her own, her dad had asked her to not think twice and "just go for it". She did and built up a great success story.

"You need to jump in, put your head down and try as hard as you can."

Chris at her home office.

Dear Ms Expat,

You never know how long you are going to be here, so you need to make the most of it. You could also move anytime and that is a great opportunity to discover and travel more. There are so many different corners of Singapore to explore. Also, Singapore is a great hub from which to travel across Southeast Asia.

Be open-minded and put yourself out there. Go do things you would normally never do and talk to people you normally wouldn't talk to! The hardest thing to do is to build your network and make your new family. As an expat, because most of us don't have family close by, your relationships with people here become quite tight. Our kids are more like cousins to our friends' kids. You can build a lovely life here.

I envy anyone who is just arriving because while it is hard and challenging, it is also lots of fun and you have so much to explore and enjoy!

Best wishes,
Chris

Acknowledgements

This book brings together multiple coffee conversations, torn-up plans, treasured memories, heart-breaking sobs, moments of solitude and immense strength. My sincere thanks to all the women (and men) across many countries who have shared these precious moments with me. In more ways than you can imagine, you've made this happen, and I hope you hear your voice in these stories.

I would like to thank my parents for giving me unwavering support through life and pitching in to manage my home, as deadlines loomed close. My husband who tolerated the all-nighters and made innumerable mugs of coffee and my little boy who ensured that all well-planned writing hours vanished without a written sentence—thank you for the sanity and the madness.

There have been many small and big contributions made by my friends and family: from sending out introductions, helping with suggestions or just listening. You know who you are and I am very fortunate to have you in my life.

My gratitude to the women featured in this book who made the time to have uninhibited and open chats about their fears, successes and dreams. And their families who supported them through their journeys.

The book wouldn't be in your hands without the support of the Marshall Cavendish family. Their support has been heartening since the very first meeting.

Thank you,

Sushmita

Acknowledgements

Heartfelt thanks to family and friends who helped at every step; to the women we interviewed for opening their lives to us; to every serendipitous moment that has led to this book being a reality.

Sincerely,

Savitha

Acknowledgements

ABOUT THE AUTHORS

Sushmita Mohapatra is a senior content and communications strategist, who has worked with firms like PwC, McKinsey & Company and Skyscanner. A former print & TV business journalist, she runs her own content marketing firm.

Savitha Venugopal is a journalist with 15 years of experience in print and digital media. She has written on gender, business, travel and lifestyle and has worked with leading newspapers in India.

Both Sushmita and Savitha have been living in Singapore since 2013.